Arnold of Brescia

Arnold of Brescia

Apostle of Liberty in Twelfth-Century Europe

Phillip D. Johnson

Foreword by Paul R. Sponheim

WIPF & STOCK · Eugene, Oregon

ARNOLD OF BRESCIA
Apostle of Liberty in Twelfth-Century Europe

Copyright © 2016 Phillip D. Johnson. All rights reserved. Except for brief quotations in critical publications or reviews, no part of this book may be reproduced in any manner without prior written permission from the publisher. Write: Permissions, Wipf and Stock Publishers, 199 W. 8th Ave., Suite 3, Eugene, OR 97401.

Wipf & Stock
An Imprint of Wipf and Stock Publishers
199 W. 8th Ave., Suite 3
Eugene, OR 97401

www.wipfandstock.com

PAPERBACK ISBN: 978-1-62564-924-9
HARDCOVER ISBN: 978-1-4982-8669-5
EBOOK ISBN: 978-1-4982-7579-8

Manufactured in the U.S.A. FEBRUARY 9, 2017

New Revised Standard Version Bible, copyright 1989, Division of Christian Education of the National Council of the Churches of Christ in the United States of America. Used by permission. All rights reserved

Cover image of Arnold courtesy Alchetron.com

Cover design by Sandy Nelson, www.SandyNelsonDesign.com

Map: Paris in 1180 printed courtesy The University of Wisconsin Press

Map of Rome in the Middle Ages Credit: Historical Atlas by William Shepherd (1923-26). University of Texas at Austin.

Photo of Piazzalle Arnaldo in Brescia, Italy by Scatti & Bagagli

Photo of bust of Arnold in Gianacola Rome by Jessica Spengler

Dedication

To Eric, Jennifer, Violet, Hazel, and Sandy

But when [Arnold] saw that his punishment was prepared, and that his neck was to be bound in the halter by hurrying fate, and when he was asked if he would renounce his false doctrine, and confess his sins after the manner of the wise, fearless and self-confident, wonderful to relate, he replied that his own doctrine seemed to him sound, nor would he hesitate to undergo death for his teachings, in which there was nothing absurd or dangerous.

And he requested a short delay for time to pray, for he said that he wished to confess his sins to Christ. Then on bended knees, with eyes and hands raised up to heaven, he groaned, sighing from the depths of his breast, and silently communed in spirit with God, commending to Him his soul. And after a short time, prepared to suffer with constancy, he surrendered his body to death.

Those who looked on at his punishment shed tears; even the executioners were moved by pity for a little time, while he hung from the noose which held him. And it is said that the king, moved too late by compassion, mourned over this.

—THE BERGAMESE POET
GESTA DI FEDERICO PRIMI IN ITALIA

Contents

Foreword by Paul R. Sponheim | ix

Preface | xi

Acknowledgements | xiii

List of Illustrations | xiv

Chronology | xv

1 Lay of the Land | 1
2 Studying with Peter Abelard | 25
3 The Community of San Pietro and the Commune of Brescia | 43
4 On the Move | 61
5 Pastor of the Republic of Rome | 84
6 Martyr | 114

Appendix I: Texts of Primary Sources | 127

Appendix II: Arnold's Student Days With Peter Abelard in Paris | 147

Appendix III: Heloise d' Argenteuil and Peter Abelard | 150

Appendix IV: Maps and Photos | 157

Bibliography | 161

Index | 167

Foreword

AT THIS TIME, WHEN the church seems urgently called to the discipline of self-examination, it is propitious to receive the resources of this courageous twelfth-century reformer.

The research supporting the thesis of this book is thorough and careful. The primary texts and crucial maps are available in appendices and are copiously referenced in the body of the dissertation. A very useful bibliography is in place. Johnson interacts with conflicting secondary sources, sifting through the evidence, and makes discerning use of his historical imagination. A guiding principle at work for him is to not go beyond what the evidence supports. He lets stand the questions that emerge from the study of this fascinating figure from the twelfth century.

Publication of this dissertation will be valuable for other students of this period. The resources gathered here will be usefully at hand for other scholars studying the medieval church. Persons specifically interested in the influential writings of Peter Abelard will be particularly grateful for the access granted through Arnold's study with this major figure.

More broadly, this window on the twelfth century will make clear that the reforming impulse was present well before Martin Luther and other later reformers who appeared on the scene of history. Johnson drives home strongly the point that Arnold of Brescia's teaching and preaching were drawn from and directed to his concern for the ministry of the church.

He tried valiantly to call the church back from the acquisition of secular power. The kind of clarity that one may find in Luther's two-kingdoms teaching is anticipated here. In the study of this theologian, martyred for his convictions, theological students can gain a sense of the life-and-death significance of the faith. They can also be led to appreciate how fully Arnold's

Foreword

teaching and preaching cannot be divorced from his life in community as an Augustinian canon regular.

Johnson's writing has an enviable clarity and will be readable by non-specialists in this period. There is a liveliness to his account of Arnold's life that draws the reader into conversation and contemplation of the reader's own need to face the contemporary moral and intellectual challenges comparable to Arnold's. Each chapter has a summary that draws matters together with admirable conciseness.

—Paul R. Sponheim
Professor Emeritus, Systematic Theology, Luther Seminary

Preface

My interest in Arnold of Brescia began when Professor Norton Downs of Trinity College stood and, glass in hand, elbow resting on the mantle of his fireplace, talked about the ferment of the twelfth century. It compared, he said, to the dynamism of the twentieth. He introduced Arnold of Brescia as one example of the excitement of a time of openness and exploration, when intellectual life had not, as yet, hardened into dogmas.

Downs told us this man Arnold was the chief ecclesiastical figure in Rome in the mid-twelfth century. During his time, in large part because of him, the pope was without access to the city. Surprised and intrigued, I began to learn more about him. Years later when I enrolled in the master of theology program at Luther Seminary in Saint Paul to study church history, Arnold was an easy choice for my thesis topic.

Now, fifty years after my class with Dr. Downs and more than twenty-five years after completing my thesis, *The Ministries of Arnaldo of Brescia*, I am exploring his life again. How do I account for this enduring interest? Why might you be interested?

The impact of Arnold's preaching, teaching, and action has had significant influence through the years. He was a powerful voice for democracy, fostered *de facto* separation of church and state in Rome while he was city pastor, decried the wealth and secular power of the papacy, enhanced the life of the laity, and was a leading participant in the intellectual enthusiasm of the first half of the century.

His reputation as an outstanding scholar and his faithful Christian life were acknowledged by foes and friends alike. Though he had no force of arms, his influence with the people was such a great threat to the medieval structure undergirding the power and privilege of pope and emperor that they joined forces to put him to death. And, as best they could, erase all memory of him.

He studied and taught with Peter Abelard, the brilliant and notorious teacher who drew floods of students to Paris during the teens, twenties, and thirties of the century. Exploring Arnold's life leads one into the fresh new world of the twelfth-century, where we meet people among whom were Heloise d' Argenteuil—scholar, prioress, and wife of Peter Abelard, Bernard of Clarivaux, John of Salisbury, Otto of Freising, Frederic Barbarrosa, and a number of popes. We enter a world of burgeoning communes and lively long distance commerce, an era peopled with serfs, nobles, clergy, wandering scholars, studious monks and nuns, and excited cathedral school students in the midst of an intellectual renaissance.

I invite you to join me on an excursion into the great twelfth-century by means of the life of Arnold, the canon regular and apostle of liberty from Brescia, Italy.

Acknowledgments

THE WRITER WISHES TO thank a few of the many people who have been helpful to him in writing this book.

First, thanks to Sandra Johnson for her thoughtful proofreading and editing of the initial document. Thanks also to Eric and Sandra for wonderful hours spent tracing the travels of Arnold of Brescia through Italy, Switzerland, and France during the summer of 1986. Thanks to friends of the Society for Pure Reason who provided funds for travel and research as well as assistance in many other ways. Thanks to Dr. Norton Downs of Trinity College, Hartford, who first introduced me to Arnold of Brescia. Thanks to Rosa Ziboli and the staff of *Civica Biblioteca Queriniana*, Brescia, Italy, for their kindness to a wandering American—especially for providing a copy of the chapter from *Storia di Brescia* about Arnold. Thanks also to the young boy from Cavacaselle, Province of Verona, who helped rescue a vital notebook from a closed and locked Mobil Station.

Thanks to my thesis advisor, the late Dr. Carl A. Volz, and the late Dr. Paul Sonnack, who provided much needed help and encouragement during Dr. Volz's sabbatical.

A very special thanks to Dr. Paul Sponheim for his support for the present project and to Karen Alexander of the Luther Seminary Library. Thanks to Mary Pattock for her indispensable editing. Errors are my own doing. Thanks, also, to Dr. Thomas Tredway who has been a colleague in conversation through the years on many matters in which he is a professional, including history, theology, and bicycles.

—Phillip D. Johnson
Minneapolis, Minnesota

Illustrations

Map of Paris in 1180 | 157
Medieval Map of Rome | 158
Piazzalle Arnaldo, Brescia, Italy | 159
Bust of Arnold in Gianicolo, Rome, Italy | 160

Websites of interest and images of Arnold can be found by searching Arnold of Brescia and Piazzalle Arnaldo among others .

Chronology of Arnold's Life

THE ORDER OF EVENTS is, for the most part, well established. Precise dating is not possible; sometimes the dates given are a best guess, marked by an asterisk.

1100*	Birth in Brescia
1114–19*	Studies in Paris
1119–39	Canon/Abbot at San Pietro Olivetta in Brescia
1139	Exiled from Italy by Pope Innocent II for supporting the Brescian commune's rebellion against ecclesiastical control of the city
1139–41	Teaching with Peter Abelard at Mont-Sainte-Geneviève in Paris
1141	Condemned with Peter Abelard at the Council of Sens
1141	Returned to teaching at Mont-Sainte-Genviève
1142	Exiled from France at the instigation of Bernard of Clairvaux; began teaching in Zurich, Switzerland
1143	Banished from Zurich at the instigation of Bernard
1143	Becomes guest of Cardinal Guido, papal legate in Passau, Bohemia
1146*	Reconciled to the church by Pope Eugenius III; does penance in Rome
	Joins in support of the Roman commune and Senate, breaks with pope
	Provides pastoral services independent of the pope

Chronology of Arnold's Life

1148	Declared a heretic by Pope Eugenius
1148–55	Enters pact with Roman Senate and becomes Pastor of the City
1149	Roman Senate offers to crown Conrad III as Holy Roman Emperor
1152–55	Senate makes offers to crown Frederick Barbarossa, Conrad's successor
1155	Pope Adrian IV imposes interdict on the City during Holy Week and demands expulsion of Arnold in exchange for lifting the interdict
1155	Arnold captured by King Frederick Barbarossa's men, turned over for trial, condemned as a heretic, hanged, his body burned, and his ashes thrown into the Tiber River so as to leave nothing of him for his followers to venerate

1

Lay of the Land

FRESH BREEZES WERE BLOWING throughout Europe as the year 1100 ushered in the twelfth century. Minds were coming alive and experience was broadening; sunshine broke through both metaphorically and climatologically. The continent was becoming warmer, the food supply increasing, and the population growing.

Europeans were traveling to distant lands, meeting people, and learning about the cultural ways of others. Thousands of fighting men throughout Europe had stopped fighting one another—their primary activity, and joined forces in a fighting pilgrimage, or Crusade, that reconquered Jerusalem and the Holy Land for Christendom.

At the Council of Clermont, November 26, 1095, Pope Urban II proclaimed:

> Let those who have formerly been accustomed to contend wickedly in private warfare against the faithful, fight against the infidel and bring to a victorious end the war which ought long since to have begun. . . . Let those who have formerly been mercenaries at low wages, now gain eternal rewards. . . . Moreover, the sins of those who set out thither, if they lose their lives on the journey, by land or sea, or in fighting against the heathen, shall be remitted in that hour: this I grant to all who go, through the power of God vested in me."[1]

---

1. Fulcher of Chartres, *Chronicle*, in Downs, Ed., *Basic Documents in Medieval History*, 74, 75.

"When Pope Urban had said these and very many similar things in his urbane discourse, he so influenced to one purpose the desires of all who were present, that they cried out, 'It is the will of God! It is the will of God!'"[2]

By 1100 the mission had been accomplished: the victorious crusaders had established the Latin Kingdom of Jerusalem. Soldiers, many with wounds and lost limbs, were making their victorious, likely weary, ways home. They returned with new knowledge from foreign experience. Commerce followed in their wake, a new economy was emerging, and the feudal system was coming apart. Travelers and traders hastened its demise.

Into the changed and changing world following this great military pilgrimage, Arnold of Brescia was born about 1100,[3] when Paschal II (1099–1118) was pope and Henry IV (1084–1105) was Holy Roman Emperor.

During the years following the First Crusade, children such as Arnold must have played crusader, pretending to be soldiers as they acted out imagined scenes drawn from tales about the lives of the heroes who conquered Jerusalem. The minds of many, young and old, were filled with stories about places in the East, the names of which their parents had likely never heard as children. The names Aleppo, Damascus, Antioch, Constantinople, and Jerusalem evoked imagination. People in twelfth-century Europe lived in the knowledge that Christendom had prevailed. For children in cities such as Brescia during the first years of the century, the world was larger and fresher than it had been for their parents as children—larger and fresher than it had been for people in Western Europe for several centuries.

This story begins in Northern Italy in the in the city of Brescia, capital of the Province of Brescia, where Arnold grew up. Brescia is located on the northern edge of the Lombard plain, in the large, flat, rich—both then and now— agricultural valley of the Po River. The Po flows eastward across Italy from the mountains in the west to the Adriatic Sea. Milan is fifty-six miles west of Brescia, Verona forty miles east, and Venice, on the Adriatic, ninety-six miles east. North of Brescia are the Dolomite Mountains and the German border.

Midway between Brescia and Verona, eighteen miles from Brescia, is beautiful Lake Garda, the largest lake in Italy. From the middle of its wide southern base, Sirmione, a peninsula made famous by the Roman poet, Catullus,[4] extends northward. Sheltered by mountains to the north, the

---

2. Robert the Monk, Ibid., 76.

3. The date of Arnold's birth is unknown. Some writers think he was born in the last decade of the eleventh century, others the first decade of the twelfth. He was probably born by 1100, or slightly earlier.

4. Catullus (ca. 84 BCE–54 BCE) loved spending time at Sirmione, as his poem,

region has a lovely climate, similar to the Mediterranean's. Olives grow in the countryside and the soft air is filled with fragrance. Fifteen miles west of Brescia is Lake Iseo, still a popular recreation spot.

Major factors to consider for getting a sense of Arnold's world are roads and travel, the developing city commnes, the papacy, empire, and reform of the church, new forms of ministry—Augustinian Canons Regular and Cisterians, and the renaissance of Latin classics, Roman law, and wandering scholars.

Roads and Travel

As trading increased, roads became more important. Europe had inherited the network of old Roman roads, many miles of which were still quite serviceable, especially in Italy. In most places the old roads provided the base and right of way for twelfth-century roads. Consistent with the importance of commerce to the Lombards, the roads of Lombardy were among the best in Europe. The value of good roads for developing commerce quickly became a matter of public interest. The church shared the desire for good roads and put some muscle into building them. For example, the Cistercians, who came into existence in the early twelfth century, were vigorous road builders. Bridges were an obvious aid to transportation and building them became a pious deed. Several lay orders, called *Fratres Pontis*, were organized for bridge building.[5]

The landowner through whose land a road passed was usually responsible for maintaining it, and was entitled to collect tolls in exchange. Clergy and university students were exempt from the tolls.[6] Roads were generally well maintained in northern Italy, but less well elsewhere. Few landowners

---

"*Paene insularum Sirmio*," shows. He called Brescia the mother city of Verona, "*Verona mater amata meae.*" Hare, *The Cities of Northern Italy, Vol. I.* 241. The Latin text of "*Paene insularum Sirmio*" can be found in Hare, 252, and an English translation in Ross and McLaughlin, *The Portable Roman Reader*, 263.

5. Thompson and Johnson, *An Introduction to Medieval Europe*, 576. *The New Catholic Encyclopedia*, Vol. 2, 789, mention two bridge building orders formed in the twelfth century, one at Avignon in 1181, and another at Lyons, in 1184. The Avignon order solicited funds for bridge building; the one at Lyons appears to have supervised construction.

6. Cave and Coulson, *Source Book*, 398. In the year 1100 there were as yet no universities.

spent money from tolls to repair the roads.[7] Medieval roads, especially outside Italy, "were little more than cross-country trails, and since they were neither graded nor drained, they were either muddy or dusty, and in any case full of holes. Bad spots were crudely repaired with rushes or faggots or boughs of trees."[8]

Roads in the early twelfth century, though better than in the immediate past, were in much poorer condition than during the days of the Roman Empire. Roman roads were built of stone, well engineered, and suitable for vehicular traffic. Julius Caesar once averaged 100 miles per day traveling from Rome over the Alps through Great St. Bernard Pass, known then as Mons Jovis, to Geneva. He traveled by *"reda"*—a two-wheeled gig pulled by a horse.[9]

More than 1,100 years later, that same pass was the main trading route to the north. Merchants from Brescia and other Italian cities would travel up the Valle de Aosta, haul their goods over the Alps by way of Great St. Bernard Pass, continue on through Lausanne and Besancon to Langres, and then on into Champagne.[10] Champagne was a rich region east of Paris in which great medieval marketing fairs were held annually. Highly organized events, they rotated among four cities: Troyes, Provins, Lagny-sur-Marne, and Bar-sur-Aube.[11]

Merchants with sufficient resources used horses and mules to carry goods, while those less affluent carried goods on their backs. Early in the century, roads were not in sufficiently good condition to transport merchandise in carts or wagons. Some people used wheelbarrows to get goods over the passes. Thompson and Johnson state the rate of travel as eighteen to twenty miles per day.[12] People traveled on the left side of the road so that the right-handed majority could have their sword arms in the best position to defend themselves from attack.

Later on, commercial traffic from Italy began to shift to the south. Merchants preferred to avoid the Alps (Great St. Bernard Pass was closed with snow seven months of the year) by using southern passes and shipping their goods up the Rhone River from southern France. An alternate route

7. Ibid., 575.
8. Ibid.
9. Von Hagen, *The Roads that Led to Rome*, 195.
10. Thompson and Johnson, *Introduction to Medieval Europe*, 567.
11. Gies, *Life in a Medieval City*, 211.
12. Thompson and Johnson, *Introduction to Medieval Europe*, 577.

to Champagne crossed the Alps at Little St. Bernard Pass, south of Mont Blanc, and followed the road west to the Rhone River at Vienne. Merchants loaded their goods onto boats, traveled up the Rhone to the Saone River, and up the Saone toward Champagne. Other merchants followed the major overland route going north toward Champagne or Paris.[13]

Pilgrims and wandering scholars, bishops, emperors, the ambassadors of popes, the popes and emperors themselves, and others who found it necessary to be on the move joined the merchants on busy roads that were getting busier during the lifetime of Arnold of Brescia.

The Developing Communes

Democratic city-states, called communes, had been developing in northern Italy for about fifty years, and rapidly by 1100. The Crusade greatly stimulated commerce leading to social and political developments that undermined feudalism and fostered communes leading to the development of cities. Perpetual struggle between papacy and empire opened the door for the success of communes and the creation of civil liberties. Cities provided passage to freedom. A person who could establish residence in a city for one year became a free man or woman. One can imagine the dreams of getting out of serfdom.

> Although traces of city institutions may be perceived earlier, it was only in the decades just before and after 1100 that the full-fledged commune appears in the *Regnum Italicum*. It was the breakdown of imperial and feudal government during the struggle of the Papacy and the Empire which gave the citizens the occasion to develop the sworn leagues of classes and whole towns which had been growing for a century, into what was in practice a republic.[14]

The idea of a democratic city-state was not new in Italy. The tradition of the glorious city-states and democratic republics of ancient times, such as Rome and the great cities of the Greeks, served to inspire and legitimate the new communes. The communes grew naturally, if turbulently, fueled by economic development. The turbulence reflected the fact that the commune was a bold new political organization and a drastic departure from the existing feudal and ecclesiastical orders of society.

---

13. Most of these places can be found using Google Maps.
14. Previte-Orton, *Cambridge Medieval History*, 545.

Arnold of Brescia, Apostle of Liberty

The German historian Otto, Bishop of Freising, uncle and supporter of Frederick Barbarossa,[15] chronicled the march of Barbarossa and his armies to Rome to be crowned Holy Roman Emperor by Pope Adrian IV (c. 1100–1159) on June 18, 1155. Otto described the Italian communes, of which Brescia was one. He had observed communes on an earlier visit to Italy in 1145 and 1146. Otto's description reveals his commitment to the imperial claims of political authority and his support for Frederick's sieges of various Lombard cities during his coronation visit to Italy. As we shall see, Frederick's campaign was a decisive event in the life of Arnold of Brescia.

Otto:

> In the governing of their cities, also, and in the conduct of public affairs, they still imitate the wisdom of the ancient Romans. Finally, they are so desirous of liberty that, avoiding the insolence of power, they are governed by the authority of consuls rather than by rulers. They are known to be three orders among them: captains, vavasors, and the people. To prevent the growth of class pride, the consuls are chosen from each class, not from one only, and, for fear that they may yield to the lust of power, they are changed nearly every year.
>
> Hence it has come to pass that, since almost the whole country belongs to the cities, each of them forces the inhabitants of its diocese to join it, and one can hardly find, within so wide a circuit, a man of rank or importance who does not recognize the authority of his city. . . . In order that there shall be no lack of forces for coercing their neighbors, the cities stoop to bestow the sword belt and honorable rank upon youths of inferior station, or even upon laborers in despised and mechanical trades whom other peoples exclude like the pest from the more honorable and liberal pursuits. To this practice it is due that they surpass the other cities of the world in riches and power; and, besides their industry, the long continued absence of their rulers beyond the Alps has further contributed to this end. In one respect they are unmindful of their ancient nobility and betray their barbarian origin; for, although they boast of living under law, they do not obey the law. They rarely or never receive their ruler with respect, although it is their duty to show him willing and respectful obedience. They do not obey the

---

15. Otto of Freising (c.1114/15–1158) wrote *The Deeds of Frederick Barbarossa* (*Gesta Friderici*), which described the first part of Frederick I's reign; he also wrote *Chronica sive historia de duabus civitatibus*, in which he depicted Augustine's two cities being brought into union in the church as the continuation of the Roman Empire.

decrees that he issues by virtue of his legal power, unless they are made to feel his authority by the presence of his great army.[16]

In the first paragraph Otto described the communes as healthy and commendable; they were, nevertheless, in his judgment, lawless. He embraced the emperor theory of rule—the view that the origin of power in the world is God. God's power flows down through a hierarchy. Each order in the hierarchy receives its authority from the order above it.[17] Both popes and emperors claimed their positions to be the first authority under God, but they did agree that all other orders of society were beneath them both. The communes refused to accept this theory, and the few who did drastically reinterpreted how it should apply. The conviction that authority comes from God up through the people to empower a ruler, rendering the ruler the servant of the people, was coming to the fore. This theory supported cities in exercising self-rule, and is precisely the conviction that Arnold held and advocated.[18]

As trade increased, more people became engaged in producing goods for sale, and cities grew. They replaced landed feudal lords as the authority over life in Lombardy. Previously, wrote Henri Pirenne, "Landed capital had been everything, and now by the side of it was made plain the power of liquid capital."[19] Thus, there arose an economic alternative to land as a means of social and economic organization.

It became possible to use money to fulfill feudal obligations as varied as bringing in the lord's harvest, repairing his castle, and presenting him with sheep's dung for agricultural purposes. Obligations such as these could now be fulfilled by paying an annual tax. Many regarded this loosening of feudal ties as an undesirable development and frequently clergy spoke out against it. For example:

> A cardinal [Jacques de Vitry] accused the communes of abetting heresy, of declaring war on the clergy, and of encouraging skepticism. An abbot [Guibert of Nogent, b. 1053] wrote bitterly: "Commune! New and detestable name! By it people are freed from all bondage in

---

16. Otto of Freising, *Deeds*, 127, 128.
17. Ullman, *A History of Political Thought*, 31.
18. Gunther of Paris, *Ligurinus*, as quoted by Davison, *Forerunners of St Francis*, 114. "He [Arnold] spread among the vulgar pernicious doctrines and filled their ears with impious words..." [that] "... government was the prerogative of the elected representatives of the people alone."
19. Pirenne, *Medieval Cities*, 158.

return for a simple annual tax payment; they are not condemned for infraction of the laws except to a legally determined fine, and they no longer submit to the other charges levied on serfs."[20]

Pirenne advanced the thesis that the development of cities was a result of the revival of long-distance trade and that merchants who led the new trading economy struggled with the old nobles and landowners for power and rights. In a critique of Pirenne's thesis, A. B. Hibbert argued the reverse—that existing nobles and landowners were among the new leaders—and that Pirenne overemphasized the importance of long-distance trade. Trade of any sort, long or short, was the decisive matter.[21]

The Gieses make this comment on the role of nobles and landowners in the new trading economy: "In Italy, where the nobility lived in towns, many nobles had gone into business, and some of them helped found communes. But the commune, even in Italy, was a burgher organization; in northwest Europe nobles, along with clergy, were specifically excluded."[22]

The question of whether nobles were engaged in or against a trading economy is relevant because there is evidence that Arnold was from a noble family. "In the matter of birth this Arnold was high born and noble," wrote Walter Map.[23]

As this story unfolds, it will become clear that although Arnold was a member of the clergy and, likely, from the nobility as well—both of which traditionally opposed communes, he vigorously supported the commune movement in Brescia. Hibbert's conclusions strengthen the likelihood that Arnold's father was a noble and a merchant. If so, Arnold's understanding of the significance of commercial interests and economic factors was informed by life in his family and community. Brescia had become independent and prosperous during the early years of the twelfth century. It had a substantial army, and although it rendered dues to both pope and emperor, was subject to neither.[24]

---

20. Gies, *Life in a Medieval City*, 17.

21. Hibbert, "The Origins of the Medieval Town Patricate," 15–27

22. Gies, *Life in a Medieval City*, 17.

23. Map, *Courtier's Trifles*, 50. "In the matter of birth this Arnold was high born and noble, in the matter of learning he was without a peer, in the matter of piety he was chief, permitting himself no indulgence in food or raiment except when the strictest necessity compelled."

24. Davison, *Forerunners* 113.

Papacy, Empire, and Reform of the Church

The ninth and tenth centuries, and first half of the eleventh was a low time for the church. By 1000 there were many "proprietary churches," which were, in effect, private property. Proprietary churches were controlled by landowners who could sell them to the highest bidder, and many non-proprietary churches were treated as if they were. Simony, the buying and selling of priestly offices, was regularly practiced. "Purchase of sees became a recognized thing: a tainted bishop infected his flock and often sold ordinations; so the disease spread until, as saddened reformers said, Simon Magus possessed the Church."[25] Simony was so much a part of the system that it was difficult for reformers to shake the church free of it.

Many clergy married. "By about the beginning of the eleventh century celibacy was uncommon, and the laws enforcing it almost obsolete. But they began to gain greater force as churchmen turned more to legal studies and as the pressure of abuses grew stronger."[26] Married priests with families passed benefices to their children just as lay people did with their property. This outcome made simony all the more troublesome.

When Henry III (1017–1056) became Emperor in 1046, he immediately made clear that he intended to bring reform to the church because he was vitally interested in the church as well as the empire. On October 25, 1046, at a council he held in Pavia, just south of Milan, he denounced simony and set his vigorous program of church reform into action.

As a result of Henry's reform efforts, the condition of the church improved in Germany during the middle of the eleventh century, but not in Italy.

> Of Rome, Desiderius, Abbot of Monte Cassino and afterwards pope as Victor III (1086 to 1087), could write, although with the exaggeration of a critic: "[T]he Italian priesthood, and among them most conspicuously the Roman pontiffs, were in the habit of defying all law and all authority; thus utterly confounding together things sacred and profane.... Few prelates kept themselves

---

25. Whitney, "The Reform of the Church," 9. Simon Magus was the sorcerer rebuked by Peter for trying to buy spiritual powers with money (Acts: 8:9–24), and it is after him the practice of simony is named. Verses 18–20: "Now when Simon saw that the Spirit was given through the laying on of the apostles' hands, he offered them money, saying, 'Give me also this power so that anyone on whom I lay my hands may receive the Holy Spirit.' But Peter said to him, 'May your silver perish with you, because you thought you could obtain God's gift with money!'"

26. Ibid., 12.

untainted with the vile pollution of simony; few, very few, kept the commandments of God or served him with upright hearts."[27]

The center of Henry's strategy was to find a good candidate and place him in the papal office. He exercised imperial power to depose Gregory VI, pope from 1045 to 1046, for simony and replace him with his own appointee, Clement II, pope from 1046 to 1047.

Following Clement's death, Benedict IX slipped into office again for his third term (1047 to 1048). He was deposed once more and Henry appointed Damasus II, who died, by poisoning it was rumored, twenty-three days later. Though the job was less than appealing, the right man was finally found in Lorraine, Bruno of Toul, a relative of Henry, who became Pope Leo IX, reigning from 1048 to 1054.

Leo brought guidance to church reform and made the papacy the source and center of it. "Church reform had begun in many places and under many leaders; its various forms had been tending to coherence in principles and supports, removal of abuses, and recognition of Canon Law."[28] Under Leo's guidance and through his vigorous efforts, including holding councils throughout Europe, people began to look to Rome for leadership in reforming the Church.

With the death of Henry III, the influence of the emperor faded. His son, Henry IV (1050–1106) was six years old when his father died. The years of Henry IV's minority allowed the papacy time to establish its independence without an effective rival.

The popes succeeding Leo IX and the core of reformers whom he had drawn together continued to provide reform leadership that kept the papacy at its center. Under Nicholas II, pope from 1059 to 1061, a major council of 113 bishops was held on April 14, 1059, in Rome. The council passed the Election Decree of 1059 specifying that the pope should be elected by the cardinal-bishops. If they needed help, they were to call upon the cardinal-clerics and then, if necessary, upon the rest of the Roman clergy and the Roman people, an indication of the persisting place of the City in ultimate matters.

The candidate was to be taken from the Roman Church unless no satisfactory candidates could be found. "The decree was not strictly kept, but the place given to the cardinals, who were now growing into a College,

27. Ibid., 21.
28. Ibid., 25.

was significant for the future."²⁹ This council, and the synods that followed in 1060 and 1061, decreed strict celibacy and the absolute prohibition of simony of any kind.

In 1073, Hildebrand was elected Gregory VII, pope from 1073 to 1085. Hildebrand first came to Rome at the request of Leo IX and served in the administration of each subsequent pope until his own election. He hoped for harmony between empire and papacy, but the activities of Henry IV led him to abandon that hope and the policies it had been based upon. He took the position that the spiritual power of the pope was supreme and the emperor was a vassal of the pope.

In principle, the questions of simony and clerical marriage had been resolved by this time. Reform was vigorously preached and the papacy carried out reform as best it could. A further issue—who had the right to make ecclesiastical appointments?

> The act by which a vassal received his land or office from his lord was called investiture. When kings and princes conferred the temporalities (lands and buildings) on bishops, they also gave them the rights of spiritual office by means of the ring and pastoral staff. The pope questioned the right of laymen to influence clerical appointments, especially the practice of laymen bestowing spiritual authority on bishops, and the dispute has become known to history as the investiture controversy.³⁰

In 1075, Pope Gregory VII decreed that "No one of the clergy shall receive the investiture of a bishopric or abbey or church from the hand of an emperor or king or of any lay person, male or female."³¹ Henry IV ignored the Pope's decree and appointed a bishop for Milan. In the ensuing argument Gregory declared Henry deposed and excommunicated.

The most dramatic scene of Gregory's papal ministry occurred in 1077. On his way to Germany to attend a council of German princes who were like minded in opposition to Henry, he expected to meet an escort in northern Italy who would take him into Germany. When the escort did not arrive, he took residence in Canossa, located between Florence and Milan, at the castle of Countess Matilda. Henry, meanwhile, braved the pass at Mont Cenis in bad winter weather to confront Gregory at Canossa. He presented himself in the countess's courtyard barefoot, in the woolen garb of a

---

29. Ibid., 37.
30. Volz, *The Church of the Middle Ages*, 103–104.
31. Tierney, *The Crisis of Church and State 1050–1300*, 51.

penitent, and there he waited for three days until Gregory finally relented and granted him absolution.

This event put the pope in a difficult situation with the German nobles he was scheduled to meet, who wanted to be rid of Henry. Although it was a tactical victory for Henry, enabling him to keep his throne, it became a powerful story of papal authority over empire. The struggle between Henry and Gregory continued for years.[32]

> As the Reform Movement had led directly to the creation of centralized government of the Church, so too it led, almost inevitably, to the contest for supremacy between the Papacy and its counterpart on the secular side, the Empire. Those ecclesiastics whom the Pope expected to be his obedient officials in the local government of the Church were already obedient officials of the Empire both in its central and its local government.[33]

The papacy had a distinct advantage in one respect; it had a more or less rightful claim to the allegiance of the clerks in Western Christendom who had been educated by the church. These clerks represented nearly all educated people, except for nuns and a new group of lay lawyers just coming into existence. Clergy and monks were the people who ran the bureaucracies and made the courts of rulers function.

However, the position of the popes was far from secure. They had to be constantly alert to preserve themselves from the Normans just to the south, from the frequently hostile noble families and people of Rome, and from the encroachments of the emperor to the north. Yet, at the same time they frequently needed the emperor's protection against the Normans and the Romans.

While remaining alert to these realities, the popes had their own territories to rule and were faced with trying to establish control over independent ecclesiastical sees such as Milan and other cities in Lombardy. In addition to these duties and hazards, a pope had to keep in touch with the Eastern Empire, the Latin Kingdom of Jerusalem, and the Eastern Church, which the Roman Church had greatly offended. During Mass at Saint Sophia, July 16, 1054, Leo IX's legate, Cardinal Humbert, placed a bull ex-communicating Michael Cerularius, Patriarch of Constantinople, on the altar—which had not gone over well in Constantinople. The pope faced hazards on many

---

32. Whitney, "Reform," 70–75.
33. Z.N. Brook, *The Cambridge Medieval History*, Vol. V, xi.

fronts; the pastor who was called to be *servus servorum dei* (the servant of the servants of God), had a heavy load.

Papal leadership of the Crusade, as well as of reform, greatly enhanced papal power and prestige in the early twelfth century. Monarchical government was assumed by both church and empire, and both civil and canon law were studied and developed to give direction.

In 1122 a concordat was reached at Worms, giving the church authority to grant all investiture. Although it did not resolve every issue between church and state, the concordat was a victory for the church and must have been much discussed among the canons regular at San Pietro, including Arnold, a young man in his twenties back from studies in Paris.

Although the pope and church had the upper hand for the moment, the struggle was ongoing. Furthermore, both pope and king had a third force to reckon with—the self-governing communes that increasingly managed civic affairs while pope and king flailed away at each other.

New Forms of Service

The year 1100 is a date for reckoning change in a number of matters. This is the case in the history of religious orders in the Middle Ages. R.W. Southern writes, "We shall certainly not be wrong in associating the stability of religious ideals before about 1100 with the relatively static society of the early Middle Ages, and the rapid diversification of religious organization after this date with the expansion and growing complexity of western society."[34]

Growing cities and the new economic order created needs for new forms of ministry. At the beginning of the eleventh century, bishops, secular clergy, nuns, and Benedictine monks provided the services of the church; by design, their ministries met the needs of a feudal society and economy. Monasteries provided libraries and schools, and monks and nuns copied, illuminated, and preserved books. Monasteries provided a place and a life for the younger sons of noble families who were without inheritance, and monastic establishments often operated separate monasteries for women who were widowed or chose to be single, become educated, or simply live a holy life as a nun.

Except for laypersons just beginning to get educated as lawyers, only clergy had enough education (given that nuns and other educated women were rarely employed in this way) to administer the affairs of secular rulers.

34. Southern, *Western Society and the Church*, 215.

Clerics were needed to manage the courts, keep records, and, to some extent, articulate policy. The church and its monastic institutions were feudal entities themselves, complete with land and serfs. The church also provided courts. "By A. D. 1100 a very large percentage of the population came under the jurisdiction of ecclesiastical courts and law."[35] And, of course, the church administered the sacraments and provided occasions for worship.

However, much clerical activity had become a source of wealth for a privileged few. In addition to simony there was also the abusive practice of appropriating churches. This meant that a monastery, for example, would become entitled to the revenues of a church that it would then administer, and for which it would provide religious services by means of a "vicarious," who was hired with church revenues. Total revenues, less the salary of the vicarious and operational expenses, flowed to the monastery.[36] Although the ministry provided by the churches and monasteries was substantial and important, even vital, harmful abuses and systemic inflexibility developed, resulting in a lack of pastoral care to new and growing needs of a changing society, primarily the cities.

A sketch of the order of clergy will be helpful here. At the bottom of the hierarchy, at the parish level, there were vicars, priests hired by canon priests to perform services paid for by "prebends"—income generated from parish tithes and rents. Next were priests and canons, including both secular clergy, those not living in monasteries, and the canons regular discussed below. In addition to parish churches there were large collegiate churches with an order of clergy attached to them. Next came the bishops who governed dioceses usually identical with the boundaries of the old Roman provinces.[37] This was the case in Brescia. Finally, between the bishops and the pope were the archbishops, or metropolitans—bishops of large cities. At the apex was the pope, the servant of the servants of God.

---

35. Volz, *The Church of the Middle Ages*, 53.

36. Peter the Venerable (1092–1156) defended this seemingly problematic practice against Bernard of Clairvaux's criticism of it in G.G. Coulton, *Five Centuries of Religion, Volume III, Getting and Spending*, 164. Peter wrote to Bernard, "Seeing therefore that monks do for the most part watch over the salvation of the faithful, albeit they do not administer the sacraments, we hold that they may rightly receive first fruits and tithes and offerings, and benefices of all kinds, since they [the monasteries] cause priests and clerics to perform the other offices that Christian folk need."

37. Volz, *The Church of the Middle Ages*, 46–50.

Augustinian Canons Regular

In the late eleventh century, clergy known as canons regular—in contrast to secular clergy—began to observe the rule of Augustine. They renounced private property, lived communally, took vows of chastity, obedience, and stability. They abstained from meat and wine and devoted themselves to *cura animarum*, the care of souls.

Leo IX, pope from 1049 to 1054, encouraged the grouping of regular canons into communities as a way to restore religious discipline and carry forward the work of reform.[38] Augustine had organized his church in Hippo in this way and had encouraged other churches in Africa to do likewise. The practice of establishing priestly communities under an order continued down through the ages, although it was not common before the mid-eleventh century. Augustine wrote the "rule" in a letter for a group of religious women, instructing them how to organize and how to deal with the daily problems and opportunities of living together. They were to have all things in common, pray together at appointed times, dress without distinction, and obey a superior.[39]

The rule was flexible and allowed for broad application. It was just the pattern needed to provide pastoral care in the changing society during the early years of the second millennium of the Christian era. Urban II, pope from 1088 to 1099, considered the canons of Augustine to be the service-oriented "Marthas" of the Church and the monks to be the "Marys." If Pope Urban was right, comments Southern:

> [T]he basic contrast between the followers of St. Augustine and those of St. Benedict lay in the extent to which the new canons sought in some humble way to repair the ruins of the world. The Benedictines had indeed brought order into whole country-sides on a grand scale, but primarily they sought to imitate a supernatural order in the midst of flux. The canons by contrast picked up the broken pieces in an already settled world. They rebuilt ruined churches; they restored religious life in broken-down or half-formed communities; they provided a framework of life for diffused religious impulses; they gathered together large quantities of misappropriated ecclesiastical tithes and applied them to religious purposes, for the relief of the poor, the sick, the infirm, and for the endowment of a modest religious life. In all these ways

---

38. Carville, *The Occupation of Celtic Sites in Ireland*, 8.
39. Southern, *Western Society and the Church*, 241–242.

they gave a new turn to the tradition of organized religion, and the large number of popes, bishops, and teachers in the twelfth century who belonged to the Augustinian Order testifies to their success as practical men.[40]

Once it began, expansion of the canons regular was rapid. The number of houses cannot be counted accurately, but they quickly spread throughout Europe between 1075 and 1125, a span of fifty years. The movement gained support from the reform element, including the Benedictine reformer, Peter Damian (1007–1073) and Gregory VII. According to J.C. Dickinson, both deserve credit for sponsoring the regular canons.[41] The hospice at Great St. Bernard Pass, founded by Bernard of Menthon (d. 1081 or 1086), is an example of early Augustinian houses established along or near the great medieval thoroughfares. Many houses were founded during the last decade of the eleventh century and first decade of the twelfth, including San Pietro in Oliveto, Brescia, in 1095.[42] Arnold was abbot of San Pietro during the third and fourth decades of the twelfth century.[43]

Cistercians

The Cistercian Order of reformed Benedictines was the other major new form of ministry. "The Augustinian canons aimed in various ways at serving the society around them; the Cistercians fled from it. . . . The canons did best in the neighbourhood of a castle or a town, or preferably both; the Cistercians flourished best on the frontiers of settlement."[44] They claimed to follow the "whole Gospel," which meant taking a vow of poverty and following a rigorous simplicity. The Augustinian motif was to follow the "apostolic life," taking for a model the Jerusalem church, where all things were owned in common.

On March 21, 1098, Robert of Molesme and twenty-one other monks abandoned the Benedictine monastery of Molesme, a daughter house of Cluny, and settled in Citeaux, in the diocese of Chalons in Burgundy. From Citeaux came the name of the new order—Cistercian. The site was wooded and swampy—a wasteland, so at first the project did not prosper. Robert

---

40. Ibid., 244.
41. Dickinson, *The Origin of the Austin Canons*, 27.
42. Ibid., 44.
43. John of Salisbury, *Historia Pontificalis*, 63.
44. Southern, *Western Society and the Church*, 250–251.

was recalled to Molesme, and two associates, Alberic and Stephen Harding, commonly regarded as the founder of the order, took over. In 1112, fourteen years after the founding, a monk named Bernard arrived with thirty followers—mostly brothers, uncles, and other relatives. Within five years nine new houses were founded, including the third, Clairvaux—of which Bernard became abbot.[45]

By 1152, the Cistercians had established 328 abbeys on frontier lands. By means of their excellent workers, they developed land, improved agriculture, and built roads. They lived under severe internal discipline, discouraged learning, practiced plain rituals, and dispensed with relics. "Their principles forced them to go to the edge of the settled lands of Europe, but the most far-sighted economic prudence would have pointed in the same direction. In an expanding society this was where the future lay."[46]

Lay brethren, known as *conversi*, were a major source of Cistercian strength. Prohibited from learning to read, they vowed not to aspire to full monastic status and provided a tremendous labor force. They outnumbered regular monks in the houses, in some cases by as many as three or four to one.[47]

These two new orders, the Augustinian canons and the Cistercians, reflected the energetic religious spirit of the period, each having the will to pursue its fresh vision. Perhaps some of the energy came from the tension between them. Cistercians were wary of learning; Augustinians prided themselves in study. Many Augustinian canons became teachers. Bernard of Clairvaux, by contrast, was a severe, outspoken critic of several of the intellectual leaders of the time, including Peter Abelard and Gilbert of Poitiers, as well as Arnold of Brescia. Many people outside the order thought Cistercians arrogant and aggressive.[48] Nevertheless, both orders opened new dimensions of religious life and ministry in the twelfth century.

---

45. Carville, *The Occupation of Celtic Sites in Ireland*, 13.
46. Southern, *Western Society and the Church*, 255.
47. Ibid., 258.
48. For a satirical description of the origin of the Cistercians written by a contemporary, see Walter Map, *Courtiers' Trifles* (*De Nugis Curialum*), 44–50.

Renaissance

The Study of Law and the Wandering Scholars

> Chronological limits are not easy to set. Centuries are at best arbitrary conveniences that must not be permitted to clog or distort our historical thinking: history cannot remain history if sawed off into even lengths of hundreds of years. The most which can be said is that the later eleventh century shows many signs of new life, political, economic, religious, intellectual, for which, like the revival of Roman law and the new interest in the classics, specific dates can rarely be assigned, and that, if we were to choose the First Crusade in 1096 as a convenient turning-point, it must be with a full realization that this particular event has in itself no decisive importance in intellectual history, and that the real change began some fifty years earlier.[49]

With this perspective, Charles Homer Haskins introduces the reader to the "renaissance" of the twelfth century. His work has stood the test of time. In 1982 Robert Benson and Giles Constable wrote: "Though more than fifty years have passed since [*The Renaissance of the 12th Century*] appeared, its audience and influence have scarcely diminished."[50] The features of this renaissance were the revival of Roman and canon law, the development of cathedral schools leading to universities such as the University of Paris, the creation of Gothic art, the activity of the Goliardi and the vernacular poets, and new translations of writings of the Greeks. Since the art of the period is an art of types rather than individuals, its outstanding individuals were relatively few.[51]

We will look briefly at the revival of jurisprudence and the wandering scholars, and in the next chapter, begin telling the story of the life of Arnold, which will lead us into the development of theology and the schools.

---

49. Haskins, *The Renaissance of the 12th Century*, 8, 9.

50. Benson and Constable, Editors, *Renaissance and Renewal in the Twelfth Century*, "Introduction," xvii. This is a volume of essays "Commemorating the contribution by Charles Homer Haskins."

51. Haskins, *The Renaissance of the 12th Century*, 11, 12.

The Revival of Jurisprudence

In the decades preceding the twelfth century and during the twelfth century itself, the study of law, civil and canon flourished. According to Haskins, it was the rediscovery of a legal method, a way of thinking about law, a jurisprudence, that enabled the study of law to flourish.

> Scientific jurisprudence disappeared with the Roman Empire, and while there are some traces of its reappearance among the Lombards of Northern Italy in the eleventh century, for most purposes it is true to say that it reemerges only in conjunction with the full recovery of the corpus of Roman law in the late eleventh and twelfth centuries. Only in Roman texts, and particularly in the *Digest*, could models of juristic method be found.[52]

Many, including Arnold, were rediscovering the greatness, wisdom, and practicality of the Romans on several fronts. They were rightfully in awe.

Stephan Kuttner points out that the revival of jurisprudence depended upon applying the devices of logic and argumentation learned through the study of the classical trivium (grammar, rhetoric, and dialectic). This is part of what he describes as:

> [T]he reality ... of an intellectual climate which became apparent ... wherever the need for organizing knowledge in a comprehensive, rational manner was felt ... a climate of desire for learning ... more than a search, rather an impassioned quest for understanding the universal order that must exist behind the accumulated, fragmentary, and often contradictory authorities of the past.[53]

The seeds that this "intellectual climate" nourished included rediscovered ancient texts. The particular seed that gave rebirth to jurisprudence, according to Haskins, was the discovery of the *Digest of Justinian* sometime around 1080, containing the thought of the great Roman jurists. It remains unknown exactly when and where the *Digest* was discovered. Kuttner conjectures that the discovery may have occurred as part of the "Gregorian Reform; more precisely, with the intense search for old texts of the sacred canons and *decreta sanctorum patrum* that was evidently conducted in the papal archives and elsewhere during the pontificate of Gregory VII." One place that fits such a theory is the library at Monte Cassino 80 miles

---

52. Ibid., 195.
53. Kuttner, "The Revival of Jurisprudence," 310.

southeast of Rome, the very first Benedictine monastery that strongly supported reform.[54]

In 1076, Pepo, the first of the Bolognese jurists, was involved in a decision in which the *Digest* first reappeared. It was cited that year in a case in Tuscany.[55] Irnerius, the most famous of the jurists of Bologna (121 miles southeast of Brescia and 66 miles north of Florence), began his work about the turn of the century and continued beyond 1125. A skillful teacher, he drew many students to his classroom, and he wrote extensive glosses or comments on the text of the *Corpus Juris*, especially the *Digest*. The successors of Irnerius for the next one hundred years or more are known as the Glossators.[56]

Legal thinking that developed through use of the *Digest* was applied to canon as well as civil law. About 1140, Gratian, a monk of San Felice of Bologna, set himself the task of collecting and harmonizing canon law. To produce his work, *Concord of Discordant Canons*, usually called the *Decretum*, Gratian used the "antithetical method of Abelard's *Sic et non*, but stressing the contradictions less and seeking to reconcile and harmonize at any cost."[57]

As the church continued to make laws, the body of canon law grew, whereas Roman civil law did not. "The Staufen emperors, Frederick Barbarossa and Frederick II, ordered the insertion into Justinian's Code of certain of their legislative enactments; but that was high politics rather than a concern for the growth of law. For the canonists, on the other hand, creation of new law in the Church was an ongoing process."[58]

"Roman law was to prove a strong bulwark of absolutism," wrote Haskins. However, some of the glosses of Irnerius expressed the view that there are limitations to imperial rights over the property of subjects. "[T]he Roman Senate, under the leadership of Arnold of Brescia, declared that Constantine and Justinian had ruled by authority of the Roman people."[59] Because Arnold seems to have had considerable knowledge of law, scholars have speculated that he studied for a time in Bologna under Irnerius.[60] This is conjecture, but conjec-

---

54. Ibid., 303, 304.
55. Haskins, *The Renaissance of the 12th Century*, 198.
56. Ibid., 199, 200.
57. Ibid., 215
58. Kuttner, "The Revival of Jurisprudence," 316.
59. Haskins, *The Renaissance of the 12th Century*, 208.
60. Davison, *Forerunner*, 113.

ture that helps place our subject in the context of his times and indicates the extent of his interests.

Haskins concluded his discussion of the revival of jurisprudence:

> Henceforth theology has a rival, and it is a secular rival.... The ecclesiastic, too, has a rival.... It was a great advantage to European royalty that, just when the clergy began to fail it, a class of educated laymen should appear, trained in law as well as in letters, from whom the expert administrators and agents of the future could be taken.... [I]t was natural that kings should turn to the lay jurist or legist. For good and ill, the lawyer had come as an active element in the world's government, and he had come to stay.[61]

Wandering Scholars

Although political struggles, war, and fairly rough living conditions continued, and much of Europe was frontier at this time, people were nevertheless out and about writing poems, singing songs, reading books, talking, eating, and drinking. It was the time of wandering scholars, or Goliards, who traveled Europe to study under teachers they had heard of and to find adventure with one another. They also wrote poetry, which flourished especially from around 1125 to 1230. Both the poems and the "order" were named after a poet, or the idea of a poet, called Golias. "Golias was a school, if you like, or an epoch, but not an individual."[62] The song of their "order" goes like this:

> We the laws of charity
> Found, nor let them crumble;
> For into our order we
> Take both high and humble;
> Rich and poor men we receive,
> In our bosom cherish;
> Welcome those the shavelings leave
> At their doors to perish.
> We receive the tonsured monk,
> Let him take his pittance;
> And the parson with his punk,

---

61. Haskins, *The Renaissance of the 12th Century*, 222.
62. Ibid., 179

If he craves admittance;
Masters with their bands of boys,
Priests with high dominion;
But the scholar who enjoys
Just one coat's our minion!⁶³

Playful satire reveals a surprising, jovial, human, and no-nonsense take on life in the twelfth century, a hearty embrace of the human comedy. Here is another song and a story.

In the public-house to die
Is my resolution;
Let wine to my lips be nigh
At life's dissolution:
That will make the angels cry,
With *glad* elocution,
"Grant this toper, God on high,
Grace and absolution!"⁶⁴

"The whole conception of the order of Golias is a burlesque on the regular orders of monks."⁶⁵ One particular parody is the Gospel according to Marks of Silver.

The beginning of the Gospel according to the silver Mark

In those days the Pope spake unto the Romans, "When the son of man cometh to the seat of our majesty, first say unto him, 'Friend, wherefore art thou come?' But if he shall continue knocking and giving nothing unto you, cast him forth into the outer darkness." And it came to pass that a certain poor clerk came to the Curia of the Lord Pope and cried, saying, "Have mercy on me, ye doorkeepers of the Pope, for the hand of poverty hath touched me. For I am poor and needy, and I pray you that ye should have compassion upon my calamity and my affliction." But they hearing it had indignation among themselves and said, "Friend, thy poverty go with thee to perdition: get thee behind me, Satan, for thou savourest not the things that be of pelf. Verily, verily, I say unto thee, thou

---

63. Ibid., 178.
64. Ibid., 182.
65. Ibid., 184.

shalt not enter into the joy of thy lord, until thou hast given thy uttermost farthing."

And the poor man went away and sold his cloak and tunic and all that he had, and gave to the cardinals and the doorkeepers and the chamberlains. But they said, "And what is this among so many?" And they cast him out, and he going out wept bitterly and could not be comforted.

And thereafter came to the Curia a certain rich clerk, fat and well-fed and puffed up, who for sedition had committed murder. He first gave to the doorkeeper, and then to the chamberlain, and then to the cardinals. And they took counsel among themselves, which of them should have received most. But the Lord Pope hearing that his cardinals and his servants had received many gifts from the clerk fell sick nigh unto death. Then the rich clerk sent unto him an electuary of gold and silver, and straightway he was recovered. Then the Lord Pope called unto him his cardinals and his servants and said unto them, "Brethren, see to it that no man seduce you with vain words. For I have given you an example, that even as much as I take, ye should take also."[66]

You and I may appreciate the Goliards' mirthful delight and imagine their comradery and the impact stories such as these had upon the oppressed among the populace. But, at the time there were many within the church who were appalled by clerical avarice and were embarrassed by such stories. The reform-minded saw these abuses as clearly as the satirists did, and were equally critical of them.

In addition to the revival of jurisprudence and the creative activity of the wandering scholars, this was a time of renewed artistic activity. In Rome, under papal patronage, there was a "dramatic burst of artistic activity. . . . After two-hundred-years barren of major enterprises, there was, above all, an extensive building and rebuilding of churches. This in turn gave new and massive scope to the 'decorative arts,' to sculpture, mosaic, and fresco painting. There was also a new flowering of book illumination, centered in Benedictine houses."[67] Much of the inspiration for artistic activity came from artwork of the past. There was a strong antique dimension to the revival.

The rediscovery of the Latin classics inspired new efforts in historical writing, a revival of science and philosophy, and translations from the

66. Waddell, *Wandering Scholars*, 162, 163. This "Gospel" is also printed in slightly different versions by Haskins, 185, 186, and by Volz, 51.

67. Kitzinger, "The Arts: Rome and Italy," 638.

Greek and the Arabic. The intellectual awakening generated by these studies touched men like Arnold, who traveled from Brescia to Paris to study under Peter Abelard, who was, perhaps, the prototype renaissance man of the time.

Summary

The historical setting for Arnold of Brescia's preaching, teaching, and pastoral care was characterized by lively change and challenge. He lived with intensity, experiencing the full impact of the matters we have discussed. In the following chapters we will see how he served his generation during a dynamic time rich with scholarly exuberance. Waddell calls it the time of the first madness, "The divine intoxication of the first league out from land":

> That first league, that first half of the twelfth century: Abelard lecturing in Paris; Peter the Venerable traveling in Spain and commissioning a translation of the Koran: Adelard of Bath in Syria and Cilicia, writing his book on natural philosophy and dedicating it to the Bishop of Syracuse; Hermann of Dalmatia translating the *Planisphere* of Ptolemy and dedicating it to Thierry of Chartres, "the soul of Plato reincarnate, firm anchor in the tempest-tossed flux of our studies": Thierry lecturing on the new Aristotle, just restored to scholarship: Paris for the first time become the patria of the mind, the rival in men's hearts of Rome.[68]

68. Waddell, *Wandering Scholars*, 119.

2

Studying with Peter Abelard

INTELLECTUAL LIFE IN WESTERN EUROPE from the time of the Barbarian invasions (400 to 500) to the revival of education in the West under Charles the Great (d. 814) and Alcuin, his minister of education, was kept alive in convents and Benedictine monasteries. To revive learning and foster education, Charlemagne decreed that every monastery and cathedral must have a school to educate young clerks. Monasteries had two schools, one for their own *oblati* and another for non-monastic outsiders.

Monastic and cathedral schools continued to provide education into the twelfth century. Cathedral schools, though important, were secondary to monastic schools. By the end of the century, however, the best cathedral schools were evolving into universities, the greatest and most famous of which was the University of Paris.[1] Arnold studied in Paris under Peter Abelard, the most famous teacher, and participated in the beginnings of the development of the university.[2]

The quality of education in Italy, especially in Lombardy, during the eleventh and twelfth centuries was better than in the rest of Europe. "In Italy education was never as completely extinguished as had been the case in continental Europe north of the Alps."[3] The educational traditions of the Roman

---

1. Rashdall, *Universities*, 28, 29.

2. Otto of Freising, *Deeds*, 143. See also Appendix I.B. Some scholars have challenged Otto's assertion that Arnold studied with Abelard as a youth. The questions raised are addressed in Appendix II and the case made that Arnold studied under Abelard in Paris about 1115 to 1118 or 1119.

3. Rashdall, *Universities*, 89.

world survived in Italy where there were lay teachers and schools in addition to monastic and cathedral schools. "It was customary for the Lombard nobility to give their sons a literary education at a time when the knights and barons of France or Germany were inclined to look upon reading and writing as unmanly and almost degrading accomplishments fit only for priests or monks, and especially for priests or monks not too-well born."[4]

During the period we are exploring, the desire for education became increasingly prominent in Italy—indeed, throughout the empire. It was a time of exuberant educational and literary pursuits. Arnold, as a boy, likely studied in the episcopal school, "one of many set up by Eugenius II [824-827], which owed its continuing existence to the reforming zeal of Hildebrand [Gregory VII, 1073-1085]."[5]

When Arnold came to Paris, he joined young students from throughout Europe. Many came to study under Peter Abelard (1079-1142) during the years 1114 to 1118 or 1119. Born in Brittany, the oldest in his family, Peter declined his inheritance and life as a soldier like his father, and chose a life of scholarship instead. He eagerly pursued his education and career, and taught in many places with much success, including Paris. He is regarded as the driving spirit that led to the founding of the University of Paris.

Abelard took delight in his reputation. Students and academics called him names such as the "Socrates of Gaul" and "*Rhinoceros Indomitus.*" Abelard had earned his reputation as a brilliant scholar and formidable debater, in part, by outspokenly challenging his teachers, Roscelin, the Nominalist, and William of Champeaux, the Realist. Prior to his arrival in Paris in 1114, he studied in Laon, north of Paris near Reims, under Anselm of Laon. While there, he successfully expounded on the book of Ezekiel to prove one could interpret Scripture and understand theology without having first been taught by a master.

Anselm took a dim view of his student's activities, and Abelard, in turn, said of his teacher: "Anselm could win the admiration of an audience, but he was useless when put to the question. He had a remarkable command of words but their meaning was worthless and devoid of all sense. The fire he kindled filled his house with smoke but did not light it up."[6] Anselm asked Abelard to leave town.

---

4. Ibid., 91, 92.
5. Greenaway, *Arnold of Brescia*, 28.
6. Abelard, *My Misfortunes* (*Historia Calamitatum*), 65 and Poole, *Illustrations*, 144.

Studying with Peter Abelard

Abelard did. He went to Paris where he became "a duly authorized master in the schools of Notre Dame, duly authorized for the first time in his career." From 1114 to 1118 or 1119, Abelard was at the top of the world: esteemed, respected, and beloved by many. Rashdall estimated there were 5,000 students and more in Paris in the early scholastic age and "[T]he centre of this huge and novel concourse was the master of the Cathedral School."[7]

In addition to the main course of his professorial life, Abelard was a popular entertainer; on Paris evenings, he sang and played his compositions in the taverns. As he acknowledged, during this exhilarating time of his life, he became vulnerable to other heady pleasures he would not have countenanced previously: "But success always puffs up fools with pride, and worldly security weakens the spirit's resolution and easily destroys it through carnal temptations."[8] And so it was that he fell in love with Heloise and she with him.

Before that, however, the eager young Arnold, son of a nobleman, reputed to be well-bred, a good student, eager for understanding, and sincere,[9] set off for Paris, anticipating new adventures. Imagine being a teenager walking across Lombardy toward the Alps, on your own, meeting people along the way, and learning something new with each encounter—adrenalin-producing and exhilarating.

After crossing the Lombard Plain to Ivrea on his likely route, Arnold approached the Alps. Following the old Roman road along the Dora Balthea River, he traveled up to Aosta, the hometown of Anselm of Canterbury. From there he hiked along the Artanavaz River to the Augustinian hospice at the top of Great St. Bernard Pass. Augustinian brothers (canons regular) provided travelers with food, shelter, and rescue service. Well-conditioned physically and familiar with the mountains, the canons of Great St. Bernard were known as exceptional athletes.

From the hospice, Arnold followed the rushing Entremont River down the mountain to the level farmland along the Rhone River. He passed around Lake Geneva (Lac Léman) and made his way by one of several possible routes to Paris. He may have accompanied merchants from Brescia on their way to the fairs of Champagne, or possibly family members since

---

7. Rashdall, *Universities*, 54.

8. Abelard, *My Misfortunes*, 65. Abelard provides a relatively full account of his relationship with Heloise. Her letters to Abelard describe her joy in their love, which she continued to treasure. A brief account of their story is provided in Appendix III, 150.

9. Map, *Courtiers' Trifles*, 51.

his father was a merchant. After walking 500 miles, he arrived in Paris. The journey had been an education and he was ready to learn more from the great Peter Abelard.

Student Life in Paris

The city of Paris was not always pleasant in the twelfth century. Foul smells frequently accosted the nostrils. Chamber pots and washbasins were emptied into streets graded such that water flowed from both sides toward the middle. When there was enough rain, the water flowed down the middle of the street, washing the filth away. It was best to ride on a horse to avoid foulness on a dry day and gushing water on a wet day. Those without horses wore heavy shoes "with very high, thick soles."[10] Since the drainage on the Cité (the Ile de France, see map of Paris) was poor, the atmosphere in the vicinity of the cloister of Notre Dame and the royal palace was often especially unpleasant.

A *chape*, or cape, was worn to protect one from water thrown out of windows from the higher floors. Because of this hazard, the practice of gentlemen walking on the outside, allowing ladies the protection of the wall arose.[11]

Pleasant smells pervaded the streets of Paris as well—the odors of baked goods, for example. Bishops and abbots maintained public ovens, mills, and wine presses through rights called *banalities*—feudal monopolies belonging to them as overlords. The breads, waffles, little cakes, and wafers prepared in their ovens, as well as meat, fruit-filled pastries, and wine were sold in streets noisy with commerce. Holmes informs us that these business people included:

> . . . menders of furs, menders of *henaps*, *regrattiers*, and so on. The *regrattiers* were vegetable and fruit merchants who could sell other things such as candles as well . . . There was an organized group of wine *crieurs* who were employed by the royal provost. These people visited the taverns each morning and learned what wine was available (*vin à broche*), and where. As they walked through the streets, they carried a bowl of wine that could be sampled, and

---

10. Holmes Jr., *Daily Living*, 101.
11. Ibid., 101.

they would beat against this with a small stick to attract attention. The taverns were obliged to contribute well for the service.[12]

Students rented rooms from landlords and landladies who lived near the schools. The quality and convenience of the rooms depended, naturally, on how much one could pay. The walls were normally covered with tapestry that hung from the ceiling, providing decoration and insulation.

Jehan de Hauteville described typical student quarters:

> They dwell in a poor house with an old woman who cooks only vegetables and never prepares a sheep save on feast-days. A dirty fellow waits on the table and just such a person buys the wine in the city. After the meal, the student sits on a rickety chair and uses a light, doubtless a candle which goes out continually and disturbs the ideas. So he falls asleep at his work and is troubled by bad dreams until Aurora announces the day and he must haste to the college and stand before the teacher. And he wins in no way the mighty with his knowledge. But through the grace of Nature and Fortune he wins a bride at the end of the poem.[13]

Things had not changed much by the thirteenth century, when John Garland wrote:

> I eat sparingly in my little room, not high up in a castle. I have no silver money, nor do the Fates give me estates. Beets, beans, and peas are here looked upon as fine dishes and we joke about meat, which is not in our menu for a very good reason. The size of the wine skin on the table depends on the purse, which is never large.[14]

The main locus of student activity was the Île and the Left Bank of the Seine. Up the hill and a bit to the east was the abbey of Sainte Geneviève, maintained, as was nearby Saint Victor, by canons regular. Later, both Peter Abelard and Arnold taught in the abbey school, Peter several times. To the west lay the abbey of Saint Germain-des-Prés, a Benedictine monastery, no longer in the forefront of education but with a fine library. Arnold could reach Saint Germain-des-Prés by turning right after crossing the Petit Pont coming from the island.

Perhaps the daily presence of these ancient buildings and other inheritances from the twelfth century make it possible for local people to more

---

12. Ibid., 80.
13. Ibid., 81.
14. Ibid.

easily imagine the texture of daily life of the past, than an American. On the other hand, the unavailability of such landmarks for an American on an ordinary day may make these matters more striking and more interesting.

Paris did not change much during the twelfth century. The map of the city in 1180 provided by Holmes (see appendix IV.A.) would be basically the same for 1115 and 1140, years when Arnold resided there. The old cathedral of Notre Dame, and the churches of Saint Séverin and Saint Julien-le-Pauvre, where the students liked to hold Sunday evening debates, were on the same sites as in 1180, though each had been rebuilt or was in the rebuilding process. Only the tower of the Abbey of Sainte Geneviève still stands. It is in the midst of the Lycée Henri-IV of the University of Paris which evolved, in part, from the abbey school.[15]

Arnold probably had two classes a day, a morning session and an afternoon class likely running from two to four. The afternoon class began with an exposition of a text, followed by questions and disputations, perhaps using Peter Abelard's draft text of *Sic et Non*. Some teachers ended the afternoon session with a brief sermon. Master Peter gave reading and writing assignments to be discussed in class the next morning.[16]

During the Christmas and Easter breaks, students were free to frolic and play. Approved frolicking included *ludi theatrales*—comedies staged at the monasteries. Sometimes wealthy patrons gave banquets at which jongleurs entertained with humorous poems, music, and acrobatics. Frolicking that ranged from less-approved to disapproved was furnished by readily available taverns and houses of prostitution.[17]

At the crack of dawn on school days, the sound of the watchman's horn from the Grand Châlelet, the tower guarding the bridge on the right bank of the Seine, woke Arnold. He probably washed with a soft soap made by boiling mutton fat in a lessive of wood ash and caustic soda. Next, he went to Mass and then to the cloister for the morning session, which lasted

---

15. The old abbey church was demolished in 1802. The Pantheon, briefly its replacement church, became a mausoleum. It was completed in 1779, the same year the congregation of Augustinians who owned Sainte Geneviève was dissolved—Bussmann, *Dumont Guide to Paris and the Île de France*, 245–248. Nearby stands the huge Bibliothèque Sainte Geneviève. The names of great scholars and persons of letters are engraved above the first floor around the outside of the building. Near the entrance, the name of Abelard occurs twice—the only name repeated, a fitting tribute to the person credited with the development of the University of Paris.

16. Holmes Jr., *Daily Living*, 115, 116.

17. Ibid., 112, 113.

until about ten o'clock. After that, time for rest, study, and the noon meal; class reconvened at two. After class, students engaged in horseplay, discussion with each other, and, if lucky, with their teacher. After the evening meal and vespers, students studied by candlelight.

Holy days were frequent; with no classes there was time for sport. People looking across the Seine from the king's palace area toward Saint-Germain-des-Prés comfortably watched games, tournaments, and dancing on the field called Pré-aux-clercs.[18]

Books could be either purchased or rented. Often tomes were collections of several works bound between wooden boards, frequently leather-covered. They were produced under contract with booksellers who hired professionals to copy them on parchment. Many monasteries engaged in copying and binding books as well. Authors often wrote on wax tablets and professional scribes copied them "off fair"—making a clean, corrected copy. Sometimes an author writing in the vernacular would dictate to a scribe.[19]

Apparently book business was fairly brisk, but not as brisk as it had been during the days of the old Roman Empire.

> A single bookselling firm at Rome could produce without difficulty, by the use of slave labor and the practice of dictation—a hundred trained slaves acting as scribes—in a day of ten working hours, an edition of one thousand copies of *Martial*, book ii; and a similar work, plainly bound, if sold at from twelve to fifteen cents, left the bookseller a profit of one hundred per cent. Horace's poems were published in separate books at intervals: *Odes, Epistles, Satires*.[20]

Papyrus had passed out of use (Marshall McLuhan contended that the empire fell because it lost the source of papyrus, interrupting the empire's great communication system), so medieval books were written on parchment.[21] Holmes reports that a Dame Constance paid a silver marc ($7) for a copy of the life of Henry I of England and that Abbot Samson paid twenty marcs ($200) for a copy of the scriptures.[22] Students usually locked books in a book chest or chained them to the desk. *Ars dictandi* by Bernard de Meun was a "best seller." It was a home course in letter-writing, containing

---

18. Ibid., 118, 119. See also page 77 regarding *Pré-aux-clercs*.
19. Ibid., 71.
20. Thompson, *Ancient Libraries*, 9.
21. Haskins, *The Renaissance of the 12th Century*, 75, 76.
22. Holmes Jr., *Daily Living*, 291, note 27.

various forms to help a person write proper letters—including a popular one to use when asking relatives for money.

Peter Abelard

When Arnold became his student, Master Peter was confidently employing his bold pedagogical method—using doubt to incite students to understanding, including understanding of one's self and one's life, and to encourage delight in learning.

Peter's father, a soldier, had loved learning and young Peter thirsted for learning above all else. There is no sign that he ever doubted his passion or regretted his decision.

> I was so carried away by my love of learning that I renounced the glory of a soldier's life, made over my inheritance and rights of the eldest son to my brothers, and withdrew from the court of Mars in order to kneel at the feet of Minerva. I preferred the weapons of dialectic to all the other teachings of philosophy, and armed with these I chose the conflicts of disputation instead of the trophies of war. I began to travel about in several provinces disputing, like a true peripatetic philosopher, wherever I had heard there was keen interest in the art of dialectic.[23]

Abelard used a draft form of *Sic et Non* as a teaching tool. In its final form, the text of *Sic et Non* is a list of 158 unreconciled contradictions concerning the faith, statements found in Scripture and in the writings of the Church Fathers that did not agree. Presenting contradictions was not completely new; *not* providing answers or reconciliation was. It was in Abelard's lecture hall and, perhaps nowhere else, that authorities were examined in this way.

Imagine Arnold, an eager, intelligent lad, about 16, reflecting on these propositions. Master Peter challenged him to examine the texts. Like other scholars, Arnold found much of the material in the *florilegia* (from *flos* [flower] *legere* [to gather]), a collection of the best extracts from larger works and compilations of the writings of patristic authors. Sometimes he had access to copies of the actual texts by authors such as Augustine. Abelard stressed critical care when using sources. This meant, for example,

---

23. Abelard, *My Misfortunes*, 58.

specifically excluding writings that Augustine later retracted, and not relying on the non-canonical books of the Apocrypha.[24]

To understand the impact Peter Abelard's teaching had upon Arnold and his fellow students during the Notre Dame years, let us consider five matters: Peter's love for the philosophers and the rabbis, the great divide between him and Augustine, his use of the *sic et non* method in the classroom, his position in the Realist-Nominalist debate, and his understanding of the function of logic.[25]

His love of the philosophers

There are many passages in Abelard's *Christian Theology* in which he praises the philosophers, including Socrates, Plato, Cicero, Seneca, and others. He could not more clearly express his appreciation than this:

> After the faith and moral teaching of the philosophers and their purpose or intention of leading the good life, let us look at this life itself. In their care for the state and its citizens we shall find that, in life and doctrine, they give evidence of an evangelical or apostolic perfection and come little or *nothing* [emphasis added] short of the Christian religion. They are, in fact, joined to us by this common zeal for moral achievement, and also by name. I mean that we ourselves are called Christians from the name of Christ, the true wisdom, and that we can also be called philosophers if we truly love Christ.[26]

Abelard reached for universality, a distinctive contribution noted by McCallum:

> We will here mention a feature [of Abelard's Christian thought] which appears to us, to give its *originality* character and value. We should note the range of observation which the author has brought into perspective. His aim is to base belief upon the conjoint agreement in thought of peoples distantly apart in space and widely separated in time. The faith of the Jewry and the legacy of Israel are claimed by him as elements in Christian thinking.... In some

---

24. Abelard, *Sic et Non*, 104. See also Bainton, *The Medieval Church*, 130.

25. All of Abelard's theological works were written after 1118. De Rijk, "Introduction", Petrus Abailardus, *Dialectica*, XXII, XXIII, demonstrates that the first edition of *Dialectica* was available in 1118. For a chronology of Abelard's writings see Sikes, *Peter Abailard*. Appendix I, 258–271.

26. Abelard, *Christian Theology*, McCallum, 62, 63.

passages he introduces into the debate even the philosophers of India.[27]

Peter Abelard's spirit was all-embracing; he firmly trusted the universality of reason. It's easy to understand how his celebration of openness aroused stiff resistance from conservatives like William of Saint-Thierry, Geoffrey of Auxerre, and Bernard of Clairvaux. These men were hardly alone—either in their day and age or virtually any other—in believing that theirs is the only true religion, the correct doctrine necessary for salvation—the only way. For them to think otherwise was heretical.

Clearly Master Peter was passionate about the salvation of philosophers and others outside Christianity who, through no fault of their own, did not know of Jesus. So passionate was he that Bernard quipped, "While Abelard sweated to prove Plato a Christian, he only proved himself a heretic."[28]

The inclusiveness of Jesus' statement to the Samaritan woman must never been far from the forefront of Abelard's consciousness, providing solid ground and more than enough authority:

> Woman, believe me, the hour is coming when you will worship the Father *neither* on this mountain *nor* in Jerusalem. You worship what you do not know; we worship what we know, for salvation is from the Jews. But the hour is coming, and is *now here*, when the true worshippers will worship the Father in spirit and truth, for the Father seeks such as these to worship him. God is spirit, and those who worship him *must* worship in spirit and truth (John 4:21–24).

Not that this requirement of spirit and truth was a burden. Just the opposite. But as we will see, Abelard's application of his conviction that reason was common to all humans and carried with it universal possibility of salvation, was declared heretical at Sens in 1141. Arnold, standing with him at that future time of the story, was condemned as well.

The Great Divide

"The current theories of Christian ethics were based on Augustine. They affirmed an original guilt transmitted by Adam to the human race. The theme of [Abelard's] *Ethics* is the elaboration of an acute revision of this point of

---

27. McCallum, ed., *Christian Theology*, 9.
28. Walsh, "Peter Abelard and John of Salisbury," 165.

view."[29] Abelard acknowledged a human tendency to evil but unlike Augustine, who thought ignorance and weakness made humans sinful even when they did not know it, Abelard said, in effect, not so; *intention* is necessary to make an act either sinful or good. *Consent* to evil makes it sin, not heredity. We will come back to this in the next chapter.

Sic et Non

Abelard probably used an early draft of his text, *Sic et Non,* as a teaching device at Notre Dame.[30] He did not attempt to settle the questions or contradictions he presented. He wrote, "Therefore it has seemed to us fitting to collect from the holy fathers apparently contradictory passages that tender readers may be incited to make inquiry after truth. . . . By doubting we come to inquire, and by inquiry we arrive at the truth."[31]

Thoughtful people may find this self-evident, and thus may not think it so remarkable. But at the time it was an explosive premise propelling revival in learning—it was new to apply critical thinking with the tool of logic to matters of faith and the study of theology in the same way one applied them to other disciplines—such as law. One can understand the excitement these questions and this approach generated among students and scholars. Abelard empowered students to challenge not merely the idea or concept of authority, but actual authorities, including the authority of their teacher—himself! McCallum writes:

> Throughout the *Sic et Non* the tone of writing is that of a thinker who is balancing divergent points of view and subtly suggesting that a further reconstruction of the matter under scrutiny is desirable. . . . No vote is cast either for one belief or the other. But the discerning reader rises from perusal . . . with an awakened

---

29. McCallum, ed., *Christian Theology,* 101.

30. Poole, *Illustrations,* 124, note 12, "It was at this time, [when Abelard lectured at Notre Dame] I am persuaded, with Cousin, vol. 2., 208 sqq., that Abelard wrote *Sic et non.* A collection such as this, of discrepant opinions from the fathers on the principal points of theology, is just what an ambitious lecturer on the subject would prepare for his own use." Sikes, in *Peter Abailard,* 81, 82. "We must indeed accept his own account of his objective in writing the treatise; he aimed only to incite others to the investigation of truth."

31. Abelard, *Sic et Non,* 103, 104. The translation used here is by Bainton, 129, 130. It is also found in Volz, 179, 180.

alertness, with a sense of a mind aware, like a water-diviner, of new springs beneath the contemporary surface of things.[32]

Abelard's fresh, creative teaching generated vigorous discussion. While some contemporaries thought his sophisticated, critical, and creative approach damaging to the Christian faith, Abelard certainly did not intend that. To the contrary, he aimed to develop a method to help Christian scholars proceed toward understanding when faced with disagreements and contradictions "among the multitudinous words of the saints." He intended to equip students with tools to defeat heresy and engage in inter-religious dialogue as he himself did in what was perhaps his last book, *A Dialogue of a Philosopher with a Jew, and a Christian*.

For these purposes, *Sic et Non*[33] provided a method.

1. We are to reserve judgment about what we cannot understand.
2. We must make sure we have the correct text of the canonical. "For example, Matthew and John say that Jesus was crucified at the sixth hour, but Mark at the third. This is an error of transcription in Mark."
3. We are not to rely on apocryphal writings.
4. We are to observe that sometimes an author is in error because he carelessly incorporated the work of someone else.
5. We must bear in mind the diversity of the situations in which particular sayings were uttered.
6. We should hold the opinion that has the most ancient and powerful authority in cases of controversy between the saints which cannot be resolved by reason [note that reason trumps].
7. We are to attribute errors of the fathers, if they are sometimes found, to ignorance not to duplicity.
8. We are to assume, if sometimes the errors are absurd, that the text is faulty, the interpreter in error, or that we simply do not understand.

Note the thoughtfulness and respectfulness of the process Abelard advanced. He was not, as some accused, a reckless scholar swinging a sword of destruction, riling up students, and fomenting heresy. Yet as this story unfolds, we will see that the influential Bernard of Clairvaux rejected this

---

32. McCallum, ed., *Christian Theology*, 106, n. 1.

33. This summary with Abelard's statements in quotation is drawn from passages of *Sic et Non* as translated by Bainton, *The Medieval Church*, 129, 130.

sort of exploration of the faith. One wonders if he read these guiding principles. If he did, he continued to consider the enterprise as soil for heresy as well as amounting to little, if anything, of importance.

Here are a few examples of contradictions from the text of *Sic et Non* that Arnold wrestled with in Abelard's classroom. Question one concerns the statement, "That faith must be supported by reason, and the contrary." Question XI examines the proposal, "That the divine persons differ from each other and that they do not"; Abelard points out that "Athanasius said there is one person of the Father, one of the Son and one of the Holy Spirit. The Father is not made, created or begotten. The Son comes solely from the Father. He is not made or created but proceeding. But Pope Leo I said, 'In the divine Trinity nothing is dissimilar, nothing unequal.'" There are five pages of quotations concerning this question, pro and con. What fun.

Question XXXII, "That God may do all things and that he may not." Abelard noted that, "Chrysostom said that God is called almighty because it is impossible to find anything that is impossible for Him. Nevertheless, He cannot lie, or be deceived, He cannot be ignorant of the future. Finally, He cannot deny Himself. Augustine said there are some things God can do as to His power, but not as to His justice. Being Himself justice He cannot commit injustice. He is omnipotent in the sense that He can do what He wants. But He cannot die, He cannot change and He cannot be deceived." [What was at stake? What motivated these considerations? A desire to understand the puzzles generated by their "knowledge" of what God was like? Do these same questions persist?]

XXV, "That the ancient philosophers believed in the Trinity or Word of God, and the contrary." (With this Abelard opened windows to see beyond historically conditioned literalism to deeper humanity.)

LXXXV, "That it is uncertain at what time of the night the Lord rose from the dead, and the contrary. Jerome says in one place that the hour is unknown and in another the fourth watch of the night."

XCVIII, "That Paul was called Paul and also Saul both before his conversion and after it, and the contrary."[34]

---

34. Peter Abelard, *Sic et Non*, Quaestio I, 113–118; XI, 140, 141; XXXII, 180, 181; XXV, 167–169. The translations of portions of XI and XXXII are from Bainton, *The Medieval Church*, 130. LXXXV and XCVIII are found in McCallum, 101, 102. McCallum, in his edition of *Abelard's Christian Theology*, 104, 105, writes concerning *Sic et Non* that it may be roughly divided as follows: "Nos. 1–22 are theological; Nos. 23–29 deal with the Holy Spirit and predestination; Nos. 30–50 concern angels and celestial beings; Nos. 51–58 are ethical; 59–84 Christological; Nos. 85–105 have instances of what

A right answer was less important than awareness of divergence and realization of the difficulties of textual transmission. Arnold, like many students of Abelard, was forced to examine his faith as he gathered knowledge of the liberal arts and theology. The exhilaration students experienced must have been accompanied at times by anxiety, fearing that this challenging, critical approach might be presumptuous, as some religious authorities charged.

The Realist/Nominalist Debate

It is unlikely that Arnold came to Paris unaware of the question of universals and particulars; it was a controversial, much debated topic. If he hadn't thought about it before, Abelard forced Arnold to face the perennial question, raised with new force by the generation of teachers preceding Abelard: What is really real? Universal ideas or particular things? For example, is the idea of beauty the really real or are beautiful objects real and give rise to the idea of beauty?

Realism had long held the day without much challenge. Realists, following Plato, said that ideas or names were real and that particular things, physical objects, were accidents, not *really real* like the *ideal form* from which particulars, referred to as emanations, were derived. Plato had taught that abstract universals existed and were the source of particulars.[35]

Surprisingly, some scholars think Plato was not entirely sure which was prior, the universal or the particular, ideas or particular things.[36] He

---

we have called 'rudimentary historical criticism'; Nos.106–116 are again ethical or deal with baptism; Nos. 117 and 118 contain a long excursus on the Sacrament of the Altar which amounts almost to a separate treatise and forecasts the discussions of Reformation times; and Nos. 119–158 are an assorted collection in which Christian moral and social customs are chiefly treated."

35. Earlier, Parmenides and his pupil, Zeno, applied logic to demonstrate that the tangible world of things is an illusion, and that it follows logically that motion is an illusion, as well. One can always subdivide the distance the arrow must fly to hit a target and, therefore, the arrow can never reach the target. In fact, the arrow can't begin its flight. In fact, there is no arrow. Most people, certainly nominalists, would agree that the *logical* predicament of the arrow is not a problem for reality.

36. Lindahl, *Philosophy and Lived Experience*, 4 1, 65: "Plato is non-committal in the question of the source of the empirical world. When pushed to formulate his view, Socrates confesses that he can but tell a 'likely story.' 'The maker and father of this universe it is a hard task to find, and having found him it would be impossible to declare him to all mankind.' Timaeus, 28, b. He seems to hold that chaotic matter is eternal; it

was, nevertheless, the fountainhead of Realism and Realism informed orthodox theology of the day. Without a monistic philosophy with God as the ultimate universal ideal, Realists thought, where could God be?

Not everybody agreed. For example, Roscelin of Compiègne questioned Realism, not in theology but in dialectics or logic.[37] Roscelin argued that only particular things are real and that names are mere sounds or words to designate things. He was a proponent of Nominalism. After studying under Roscelin, Abelard went to Paris and became the student of one of the leading Realists of the day, William of Champeaux. While a student, Peter challenged both teachers, and by the time he left off teaching dialectic to study theology in 1113 or 1114, he had propounded a very satisfying synthesis—one could even say, a modern common-sense synthesis.

The synthesis is called "Conceptualism." Abelard refused to accept the extreme or final conclusion of both positions. He *did not* accept the Realists's conclusion that if the names or ideas were the real, particulars were not; *nor* did he accept the Nominalists's conclusion that if particulars were real, then names or ideas were not. Particular things *are* real, according to Abelard, *and* humans have minds that can think of ideas or concepts. These ideas or concepts are real and actual as the person, one's self, thinks them. "If the universals, if abstractions of all sorts, were the creations of the intellect, they were also its necessary creations; they were therefore so far real that the human mind could not do without them."[38]

L. M. De Rijk argued, in his introduction to Abelard's *Dialectica*, that "Enough emphasis cannot be laid on the fact that this *logical* Nominalism is not such as to exclude Abelard from the way to a *philosophical* Realism. By the latter term the school is meant that starts from the view that (1) there are extra-mental things, the existence of which is independent of the human mind, and that (2) man is capable, to a certain extent, of knowing them."[39]

This seems upside down. How would anyone *know* something extra or *beyond* mental that is independent of people's minds? According to De

---

becomes as the Demiurge gives it form." Also to the point is Abelard's reference to the Timaeus: "The Craftsman of the universe, and its begetter, is hard to find, and even when found, difficult to define." *Christian Theology*, 68, 69.

37. Roscelin's doctrine had been condemned by a council of Soissons in 1092. It must have been after this that Abelard, as a very young man, was his student. Poole, *Illustrations*, 117, note 3, says Roscelin, "appears to have submitted to the sentence and to have been allowed to hold a scholastic post at the church of Saint Mary of Loches in Touraine."

38. Poole, *Illustrations*, 120.

39. De Rijk, "Introduction", *Dialectica*. XCIII, XCIV

Rijk, humans are, nonetheless, capable to a *certain extent* to know them. Relying on Poole's understanding of Abelard in his *Illustrations*, universals and abstractions of all sorts are necessary creations of the intellect. This means these conceptual realities are created by the active human mind of the child and the rest of us. This contrasts with the philosophical realism of De Rijk in which the extra-mental realities are independent and somehow knowledge of them seeps down.

De Rijk considered mistaken the notion that Abelard's synthesis can be called conceptualism. "By not distinguishing Abelard's logical nominalism from his philosophical realism, Cousin and other French historians seem to have arrived at their theory of Abelard's 'conceptualism.'"[40]

It is questionable whether distinguishing the philosophical from the logical would have convinced scholars like Poole that they were wrong to think of Abelard's synthesis as Conceptualism. Do not most people think the map is not the territory and the word is not the thing? And yet, when a less-than-two-year-old looks at a ball and says the word "ball," she knows the *word* "ball" represents all balls, of which there are more. Likely the child resolves wordlessly to watch for balls and, when coming across one, enjoys her ability to recognize it as ball. Does the child think the concept of ball is a real thing? Is the word ball a thing? It is a sound. That's real. The idea of the ball is immaterial and real. Does it exist independent of people thinking it? De Rijk says that it does, and insists that Abelard thought so, too.

Conceptualism arose when Abelard rejected the extremes of both Realism (that only universal ideas are really real), and Nominalism (that only particulars are really real). He believed both ideas and particulars to be real.

We have touched on the Realist-Nominalist debate in a few paragraphs; in the early twelfth century it filled entire books, and hours of lectures and discussions. Surely Arnold spent many hours thinking about this matter as a student, and, under the guidance of Abelard, applied the insight gained to shed light on all areas of life, including theology.

The function of logic

Dialectia or *logica* is the art that aims at distinguishing valid arguments from invalid ones and is limited to that. De Rijk informs us that in the treatise, *Logica Nostrorum petitioni*, "Abelard here points to the fact that logic is not a theory of thought, which teaches us how we ought to think

40. Ibid.

and dispute: its only function is to distinguish valid arguments from invalid ones and to state why (*quare*) they are valid or not."⁴¹

Abelard's *Dialectica* is an example of his rigorous, logical thought. He had developed the ability to think objectively. For him, objectivity was a matter of perspective. Objectivity was served well by the sort of discipline he gained through formal study of logic such as taught by Roscelin.⁴² Convinced that all questions could and should be approached objectively, Abelard proclaimed the importance of reason, its personal utility, and its universality in humans. Reason required objectivity, it was a wonderful gift given to humans only, and it was the clearest evidence that humans were created in the image of God.

He did not consider reason more important than faith. Reason as an objective approach could not be set aside, and faith was the given material upon which reason worked. Faith had content; it included the scriptures, the teachings of the fathers, and other forms of revelation such as nature—realities that could be fruitfully examined with the aid of the teachings of philosophers. Philosophy was the critical application of reason to the body of Christian faith. Accusations by his opponents that he placed reason above faith were inaccurate; nonetheless, misunderstanding persisted.

Arnold gained a powerful tool from his training in logic. Like the method of *sic et non*, logic freed the scholar and theologian to question, learn, and discover new things and come to new understandings. Arnold needed intelligence, objectivity, and rigorous scholarship to complete his education, equip him for his calling, and qualify him to become a colleague of Peter Abelard years later.

In addition to logic, Arnold studied the other two subjects of the *trivium*, grammar and rhetoric. Grammar included Latin language and grammar, but was primarily the study of Latin literature. The standard textbook was *Institutiones* of Priscian of Caesarea, composed in the sixth century. This large volume included substantial quotations from Latin authors such as Cicero, Sallust, Virgil, and Terence.⁴³ Haskins wrote, "At its best the study of grammar in the twelfth century carried with it the serious

41. Ibid., XXIV.

42. Because Abelard does not mention Roscelin in *Historia Calamitatum*, some scholars have challenged whether, in fact, he was a student of the Nominalist logician. It was Otto of Freising who made the statement (*Deeds*, 83). Otto's information has been confirmed by the publication of a letter from Roscelin to Abelard. See Poole, *Illustrations*, 130 and 315, 316.

43. Haskins, *The Renaissance of the 12th Century*, 130 ff.

study of literature."[44] In the Middle Ages, rhetoric, the third subject of the *trivium*, was devoted primarily to letter writing rather than oratory, as in the classical past.[45]

Music, geometry, arithmetic, and astronomy were the subjects of the *quadrivium*. Medicine, law, and theology—the queen of the sciences, were outside the liberal arts.[46] We do not know to what extent Arnold studied subjects of the *quadrivium*. He did not study them with Abelard. He did study theology and may have studied law.

Summary

Student days in Paris must have been satisfying for Arnold. There were other prominent teachers in the city besides Abelard. Visiting lectors and public defenses by teachers were available to students as well as discussions and lively debates. It was an exciting time to be a student. As Waddell wrote, it was the time of "[T]he first madness, 'The divine intoxication of the first league out from land.' That first league, that first half of the twelfth century."[47]

Arnold probably continued to study in Paris until 1119 or 1120,[48] even after Peter Abelard left Notre Dame. By the time Arnold left Paris and returned to Brescia, he had gained an excellent education. He loved learning and was known for learning and scholarship his entire life.

How did Arnold react to Abelard and Heloise and the trouble created by their affair? Apparently he continued to admire and trust Abelard because, as we shall see, he sought him out again twenty years later.

For now, he was prepared to go home to Brescia and take up his vocation.

---

44. Ibid., 135.

45. Ibid., 138.

46. The great universities that came into existence in the twelfth century were each known for one of these disciplines. Palermo was noted for medicine, Bologna for law, and Paris for theology.

47. Waddell, *Wandering Scholars*, 119.

48. Greenaway, *Arnold of Brescia*, 41.

3

The Community of San Pietro and the Commune of Brescia

Arnold crossed the Alps to Italy in about 1120, heading home from school. He entered the Augustinian House of San Pietro in Olivetto, founded in 1096, which became his home for twenty years.

Two influences converged upon Arnold that helped clarify and strengthen his convictions and practice. First, his religious order with its rule dedicated to evangelical precepts and learning, including study of classical Latin literature. Second, the *patarin* of Brescia who were intent on forming a commune hankering back, however loosely, to the republican Senate of Rome as its model for rationale and direction.

Study, pastoral care, and worship were the center of daily life. The canons read the rule weekly. Arnold's study of Scripture shaped his vision of the church and Christian living as in the Jerusalem church in Acts 2. The people of "the way," provided the model, and study of the classics deepened his understanding. Peter Abelard had praised the lives of the philosophers for the moral value they gave to family and community life.[1]

The records of Brescian history during this time are sparse. There are no known records from San Pietro and there are only a few entries in the *Brescian Chronicles*.[2] The material for the picture we draw of Arnold and the Brescian situation comes primarily from remarks made by the core sources

---

1. Abelard, *Christian Theology*, 59–64.
2. Greenaway, *Arnold of Brescia*, 13. "The local annals, though written in the thirteenth century, are, it is true, dated in the eleventh century, and the total number up to the middle of the twelfth comprise merely a couple of pages in the printed edition."

(most of whose comments about Arnold are found in the appendix) and the history of the times that amplifies our picture. Arnold's scholarship and dedication made him a well qualified leader and he became abbot.[3] The canons probably enlisted him to become abbot early on; educated talent was needed and eagerly sought.

As abbot of San Pietro, Arnold had an important position in the city of Brescia. Robert of Burneham, as related by Walter Map and as accepted by Alfieri, said Arnold's family was influential in Brescia, giving him added stature in the community.

Alfieri, Brescian historian, begins his account of Arnold with these words, "Arnold of Brescia, whatever his social condition and wherever he completed his studies, was essentially a Lombard *patarin*."[4] Alfieri focuses on the secular impact of Arnold's life as prophet of social change. However, Arnold did not become a prophet simply because he was a *patarin*; he was, first and foremost, an Austin canon, a passionate follower of Jesus, and a lover of truth and learning. His passions and abilities were clear to all.

In chapter 1 we discussed briefly the development of the Augustinian canon regulars (also referred to as Austin Canons). From a social-historical point of view the seeds were present from before the time of Augustine, and its development was organic. Augustine gathered his clergy at Hippo[5] and instituted common life. This was not the first time common life had been implemented, but it became a famous example. Nevertheless, the practice of secular clergy living the full common life was not widespread after Augustine's time.

> From time to time some of these institutions [collegiate churches from the sixth century on] adopted the full common life established by St. Augustine and familiar to later ages, especially through the lesson in his office that told how he "instituted a family of religious who had common food and common worship, and he taught them diligently the discipline of the apostolic life and doctrine." Clerks thus living the full common life might be called *monachi* in the same way as those living under a specific religious rule, and foreshadow somewhat vaguely the regular canons. But these earlier manifestations owed no special allegiance to St. Augustine, were

---

3. John of Salisbury, *Historia Pontificalis*, 63. Appendix, I.A., 128.
4. Alfieri, *Story of Brescia*, 593.
5. Modern Annaba, Algeria.

very seldom termed *canonici regulares*, and never seem to have succeeded in establishing a firm tradition.[6]

Houses of canons regular that formed in the tenth and early eleventh century had pretty much the same idea as Augustine, but did not adopt his rule specifically. They thought of their roots as going further back, to the apostolic community of the book of Acts. For them, Augustine was but one among a number of great Church Fathers who promoted the common life. The movement to initiate, encourage, support, and organize regular canons came from the Gregorian Reform of the eleventh century. "The need for a return to the life of the primitive Church was, as has often been noted, the whole burthen of Hildebrand's [Gregory VII (c. 1015–1085)] song, and he shares with [Peter] Damian [c. 1007–1072] the credit of sponsoring the regular canons."[7]

There was opposition to the regular canons as Dickinson informs us:

> It was easy for anyone with a smattering of Greek and Latin to wax critical over so odd a phrase, and certain Benedictines of the first half of the twelfth century took the chance with both hands. Hugh of Amiens (d. 1164) writes superciliously of "those clerks who *superjecto nomine* are called regular canons. . . . To be called 'regular canons' is just the same as to be called 'canons canons.'" Rupert of Deutz, with his fine eye for the obvious, pointed out that regular canons were "regular regulars."[8]

By the twelfth century, however, regular canons living the common life were plentiful and were doing so under the Rule of Augustine. Dickinson puts the matter clearly:

> Thus, when in the early twelfth century certain Benedictines, inebriated by the increasingly legalistic spirit of the age, opened fire on the position of the regular canons, the enormous prestige of St. Augustine and his special connection with the order offered a strong line of defence. . . . In these disputations the regular canons naturally drew increasingly on the prestige of Augustine, whom the historiography of the age enabled them to claim as founder

---

6. Dickinson, *Origin of the Austin Canons*, 13. For example, Eusebius of Vercelli, bishop from 340 to 371, lived with his clergy under rule and has sometimes been regarded as one of the founders of the canons regular. This was pointed out to me by Dr. Carl A. Volz.

7. Ibid., 13.

8. Ibid., 61.

> with some show of reason, and who held a dazzling array of qualifications which Benedictines would find hard to over-trump. Augustine, saint, theologian, doctor, bishop, and religious, was a formidable figure....
>
> A final factor must be borne in mind—the excellence of the Rule. The over-practical mind of our own day is too liable to think of the Middle Ages as an ill-instructed and impracticable epoch. To assert, as is sometimes done, that the regular canons adopted the Rule of St. Augustine largely from strategic reasons is grossly to misconceive the situation.[9]

The rule has a difficult textual history. The text appears to be derived from Letter 211 by Augustine which contains his instructions to a household of nuns whose community life had been undermined by dissensions. This has been known as the *Regula Sororum* and from it a version for men was drawn up.[10]

Common life, rather than poverty, was the controlling idea. The first Christian community, as described in Acts, was not necessarily poor. Indeed, at least at the beginning the Jerusalem community appears to have had sufficient resources. Out of common resources, community goods were distributed to each according to need. The rule is clear about this and explicitly states its implications:

> Among you there can be no question of personal property. Rather, take care that you share everything in common. Your superior should see to it that each person is provided with food and clothing. He does not have to give exactly the same to everyone, for you are not all equally strong, but each person should be given what he personally needs. For this is what you read in the Acts of the Apostles: "Everything they owned was held in common, and each one received whatever he had need of (Acts 4:32; 4:35)."[11]

The first precept states the purpose of the rule. "Before all else, live together in harmony (Ps. 67 (68):7), being of one mind and one heart (Acts 4:32) on the way to God. For is it not precisely for this reason that you have come to live together?"[12]

---

9. Ibid., 69, 70.

10. Ibid., 20 and 258. Appendix I, "The Rule of St. Augustine: Its Textual History" is found on pages 255–272.

11. *The Rule of Saint Augustine*, 11.

12. Ibid.

The Community of San Pietro and the Commune of Brescia

The vow rejecting personal property was not unique to the Augustinians. The Benedictines and the Cistercians made the same vow. The Augustinians, however, remained in the world in ways the other two did not. The Augustinian canons engaged in pastoral ministry, usually in cities. They remained in the world to serve the world directly.

Canons vigorously opposed the great wealth that churches and monasteries had amassed and expressed anger when the clergy of these institutions held on to their wealth tenaciously even when people and communities around them suffered deep poverty. Arnold declared that monastic communities in which foreswearing personal property led to extraordinary personal ease were a hypocrisy. How could churches and monasteries who expended their energies on maintaining wealth and property rather than focusing on ministry, and that fought to maintain and increase, rather than relinquish, their political authority, represent Jesus and Christian living? For Arnold, refusing to let go of wealth and power, particularly temporal power, contaminated the church of Jesus Christ, and he was deeply disappointed that church reform had thus far failed to change this. Consequently, the traditional reform movement no longer held promise.

Alfieri sums up Arnold's position:

> That the church, especially among its leaders and in its highest hierarchics, after having encouraged, planned, and directed a stately movement for the regeneration of itself and of all Christian society, calling upon it to collaborate down to its most humble levels, had been distracted, as a result, by political calculations and worldly interests, was inconceivable to him; inconceivable that in the brief passing of seventy years (the life of a man), numerous were the times spent going from intransigence to compromise and compromise to intransigence in a question that he believed to have been already explicitly resolved by the "give to Caesar" in the Gospel: all the spiritual power and that only to the priesthood, and all the temporal power and that only to the kingdom.[13]

By the time Arnold joined San Pietro, the canons regular of St. Augustine were more than local communities. They were becoming an international order intent on serving the world as well as their individual parishes, and they intended to be at the heart of reform and renewal in the church.

Reform floundered. Too often centers of power protected their possessions which led to strife among the people. As Arnold saw it, popes,

---

13. Alfieri, *Story of Brescia*, 593.

many bishops, and many monks simply ignored the injunction to give to Caesar what belonged to Caesar. He harked *back* to the Roman Republic and he *anticipated* Martin Luther and secular thinkers such as James Madison who understood the need to separate religion from the secular order. It is interesting that the other two major religions, Islam and Judaism never separated civil and religious life. Their religious origins were inseparable from daily, civic life.

The difference between Arnold and the *patarin* of his home town was that Arnold had no secular ambitions. He did not aspire to be a consul or gain economic or political advantage. As a citizen, he supported the *patarin*, but he became a spokesman for the commune primarily because of his opposition to ecclesiastical control of the city.

Reform in Brescia

There is a note in the Brescian Chronicles recording the visit of Innocent II (pope 1130–1143) in 1132 when he deposed Bishop Villanus, who had been appointed by the anti-pope Anacletus. Innocent appointed Manfred in his place. "1132. *Innocentius papa Brixiam venit et eiecit Villanum de episcopatu.*"[14]

Innocent II, a reforming pope, put Manfred in office to carry reform forward. Affairs were complicated by papal schism from 1130 to 1138. Innocent's papal claim was challenged by Peter Leon, Anacletus II, who, in 1130, took control of Saint Peter's Basilica and most of the City of Rome. This forced Innocent to leave Rome shortly after each of them claimed to be elected. The Western world was divided over who was, and who truly should be, pope. The party of Innocent gained control of Brescia. The struggle for the papal "throne" weakened respect for the papacy in Brescia, as elsewhere.

Surely Arnold met Innocent in 1132. Poole states that Innocent resided in the city at least long enough to assess the situation and establish a new man as bishop. In handling this matter, he must have met with Arnold, a respected religious leader, the abbot of San Pietro. It could be that Innocent resided in Brescia for a more extended time, given that the anti-pope controlled Rome.

---

14. Frugoni, *Arnold da Brescia*, 7. He quotes the *Annales Brixienses* in M. G. H., SS., XVIII, 811.

Manfred, Brescia's new bishop, supported reform. In the shifting tides of Lombard politics, persons of the commune, such as the politically reformist *patarin*, were initially in support of Manfred and the papal party in its struggle with the Archbishop of Milan and the German kings for authority over the parish of Milan and the parishes of Lombardy.

The king of the Germans retained the right of investiture in Lombardy until 1122 and the bishops of Milan, who were in apostolic succession through the Great Ambrose (339–397), were disinclined to grant much authority to Rome. This was not to the liking of the commune of Brescia, because the archbishop of Milan claimed independent autonomy over the city of Milan, *and*, through his subject bishops, authority over the cities of Lombardy, including Brescia. Brescia preferred the pope as overlord to the bishop of Milan.

Simony remained common throughout Lombardy, abuses were prevalent in many areas, and the objectives of the communes were blocked by non-reformist archbishops and bishops who more often than not had vested property interests. So, during the early years of the reform, the goals of the communes usually coincided with the aims of the papal party. The regular canons in Brescia were products of reform, and had been supporters of the papacy from the beginning.

But as things unfolded, ecclesiastical control of the city, whether by the archbishop of Milan or the Bishop of Rome, became unsatisfactory even though the community of Brescia, including the canons at San Pietro, were pleased with reforms that had been accomplished. Opposition to Bishop Manfred grew as the inherent conflict between the *patarin* and the Prefect, a civil official appointed by the bishop, unfolded and reform faltered. The Prefect's municipal governing authority included regulation of commercial activity, most unsatisfactory to the *patarin*.

It became increasingly clear to supporters of civil reform that the policies generated by vested interests of clergy permeated the church right up to the papacy and such interests were detrimental to reform and self rule.

The conflicts between emperor and pope and leadership conflicts within each realm added fuel to the desire for self-governance. The schism in the church was matched by a schism in the empire. Lothar II (1075–1137), crowned Holy Roman Emperor, was challenged by Conrad of Hohenstaufen (1093–1152). Both the popes and the emperors were hard pressed to establish control. Avoiding hostile cities, Conrad III and Innocent II carefully made their way to Rome in 1138. Once there, they were able to arrange a coronation in the Lateran, but Anacletus, the anti-pope, remained in control of Saint Peter's and most of the City.

As limited as their success was, Conrad and Innocent would likely have accomplished nothing without the support of Bernard of Clairvaux.[15] Bernard, in spite of his professed reluctance, was almost continuously on missions on Innocent's behalf during the schism. He made two trips to Italy and traveled extensively in Gaul.

When on one of these missions in 1135, he wrote the monks of Clairvaux, "Your own experience can tell you how much I am suffering. If my absence is irksome to you, you can be sure it is much more so to me. You are suffering from the absence of one person, but I am suffering from the absence of each and all of you, and this is something quite different and much more hard to bear."[16]

Milan preferred Anacletus and opposed Innocent until Bernard went to the great city and preached Innocent's cause as the cause of Christ. A delegation from Milan had approached Bernard on his way to a council called by Innocent in Pisa in 1135. They told him that Archbishop Anselm of Pusterla, a supporter of both the anti-pope and Hohenstaufen, had been driven out of the city and they asked Bernard to help reestablish order.

After the council concluded, Bernard responded to their request. He preached so successfully that he not only won the support of the people of Milan for Innocent and Conrad, he also enlisted their help in stripping the churches of their rich ornaments.[17] In addition, he established a Cistercian Monastery in the neighborhood at Chiaravalle, "a daughter house of Clairvaux to shine as a perpetual reminder of his visit and to be a living source of spiritual strength."[18]

By this time the people in Brescia were rebelling against Bishop Manfred. In 1135, they elected two counsels and took control of the city. Villanus, the former bishop, and some of his supporters tried to regain the office of bishop. They failed, and the citizens successfully wrested control of the city from Manfred's ecclesiastical party.

15. Balzani, "Italy, 1125–1152," 363–365.
16. Bernard of Clairvaux, *Letters*, 144:212.
17. James, *Bernard of Clairvaux*, 120. "When he had restored peace and order Bernard turned his attention to the gorgeous churches of the city and induced the people to strip them of their rich ornaments. It is difficult to understand his purpose in this for, in his *Apologia*, he expressly recognizes the need of decoration in secular churches; it was only for monks that he believed it inappropriate."
18. Ibid., 121.

We can't be certain of Arnold's role in 1135, but by 1138 he was definitely supporting the commune. John of Salisbury wrote: ". . . when the bishop was absent on a short visit to Rome [Arnold] had so swayed the minds of the citizens that they would scarcely open their gates to the bishop on his return. For this he was deposed by Pope Innocent and expelled from Italy."[19]

Arnold's Convictions

Descriptions by the witnesses of Arnold's preaching and teaching are consistent. Drawing primarily from them we learn that his main themes were 1) accepting the rule regarding community goods, 2) relinquishing temporal power by the church and clergy, 3) elevating the laity, and 4) teaching on the sacraments of baptism and communion.

We suspect an ongoing connection between Arnold and Peter—not by correspondence, perhaps, but likely by word of mouth via friends, cannons, and fellow students. This conjecture recommends itself, primarily because the two became colleagues in 1139. Also, Abelard's books were available to Arnold. Many readers may experience just such a relationship with valued former professors—connections that are not lost even while there is little or no contact.

Looking at the list of Arnold's themes, we see one that we know was dear to the heart of his teacher—the explicitly theological matters of baptism and communion. Not that Abelard lacked interest in matters such as the laity, vows, and politics; but they were not his passion. Nonetheless, Arnold's vocation was imbued with Abelard's perspective.

Accepting The Rule Regarding Community Goods

Arnold and his brothers read *The Rule of Saint Augustine* weekly.[20] The purpose of life under their rule was to form a community of love centered in the love of and for Jesus Christ.

> "See how pleasant it is for brothers to live together in unity" (Psalm 133:1) . . . Only those in whom love for Christ is perfect truly live together in unity.

---

19. Poole, "Introduction," *Historia Pontificalis*, lx. See also Appendix I.A., 128.
20. *The Rule of Saint Augustine*, 24.

> Those who live in unity in such a way that they form but one person are rightly called "monos"—one single person. They make true to life what is written, "of one mind and one heart", that is, many bodies but not many minds, many bodies but not many hearts (Sermon on Psalm 132 [133]).[21]

The brothers of San Pietro renounced personal property as an expression of love for Jesus and their neighbors, to free themselves of the burdens of property, and to build up one another. Augustine regarded voluntary simplicity in material goods as a matter of laying aside the burdens entailed by responsibilities for such things, enabling one to be free for service and for spiritual life and community life. He wrote:

> But where can we find this perfect simplicity which is absolutely unwavering in unshaken perseverance: In the programme of life that I have already mentioned, namely: "He who does not renounce all that he owns cannot be my disciple" (Luke 14:33). This seems hard, but the word of God flatters no one. Many people have put this into practice.... Many Jews in Jerusalem sold all that they possessed and laid the proceeds at the feet of the Apostles.[22]

Augustine's convictions about common life ran deep. He did make a concession to his fellow bishops, who opposed his insistence that those whom he ordained to the higher grades of ministry should renounce private property: he officially permitted his clerks to live outside the episcopal house with their own incomes. He made it clear, however, that this was done for reasons of expediency rather than conviction. In sermon 355 he said, "The clerk who gives up the monastic life is half lost." He followed this with Sermon 356, in which he said that none of his clerks who were in full common life should abandon it on pain of being removed from the list of clergy.[23]

Arnold knew, from the biography by Possidius, that Augustine "showed little interest in the material things which the Church held or possessed." In fact, Possidius wrote, "If the funds of the Church became exhausted, he [Augustine] made it known to the Christian people that if there was nothing for the relief of the poor, and if necessary, he would even order the sacred vessels to be broken up and melted.... In great necessity,

---

21. Ibid., 44, 45. Raymond Canning, OSA, quotes from Augustine's sermons on the Psalms in his commentary on the *Rule*.

22. Ibid., 48.

23. Dickinson, *Origin of the Austin Canons*, 11, 12.

Ambrose, of venerable memory, did not hesitate to do the same, as he himself related."[24]

The writings of Augustine and the church fathers, the actions of the great reformers of the late eleventh and early twelfth century—men like Peter Damian (1007–1072) and Gregory VII (c.1015–1085), and scripture provided strong support for Arnold's commitment to apostolic poverty and his convictions about wealth. No doubt John of Salisbury had this in mind when he reported, "[Arnold] said things that were entirely consistent with the law accepted by Christian people," and adds, "but not at all with the life they led."[25]

Relinquishing Temporal Power by the Church and Its Clergy

Arnold's conviction that temporal power belonged to Caesar, not the church, must have deepened as he observed how political problems consumed the pope's energies and how resistance from the pope, the bishop of Brescia, and bishops throughout Lombardy to democratic communes commanded their attention, leaving little time for ministry, study, and worship. It became so obvious and fundamental to him that he could scarcely understand another point of view. Through his preaching he gained the reputation that "Wherever he lived [he] prevented the citizens from being at peace with the clergy."[26]

The word reputation is carefully chosen. John of Salisbury wrote: "He was *reputed* [emphasis mine] to be factious." We must remember that people opposed to Arnold wished to deny that there was *anything* constructive in either his teaching or ministry. John is clearly aware of this prejudice. Otto of Freising, far from objective, and fearful of Arnold's broad-reaching influence, accused him of "hatred for the honors paid to the Church," and wrote that "he assumed the religious habit that he might deceive the more."[27]

During the later years of Arnold's two decades of providing pastoral care at San Pietro, he took a stand against his bishop. He had preached and taught about issues of ecclesiastical power prior to becoming actively

---

24. St. Possidius, *The Life of Saint Aurelius Augustine*, as printed in *The Augustinians from St. Augustine to the Union, 1256*, 26.

25. John of Salisbury, *Historia Pontificalis*, 64. See also, Appendix I.A., 128.

26. Ibid., 63 and Appendix I.A., 128.

27. Otto of Freising, *Deeds*, 61 and 143. See also Appendix I.B., 129, 130.

disobedient. Had he attempted to take charge politically in some way, he would have violated his own principles. Alfieri observes:

> Thus the supporters, or at least that part of the population that wished for even greater autonomy for the commune (which would have ended up, in the long run, with the upper hand), clashed with the bishop and found in Arnold's preaching, *that probably did not exceed the moral and religious sphere* [emphasis added], a justification and thus, a consensus and, lighting their spirits, an incentive, given the intellectual stature of the man and the exemplarity of his life, which was even sincerely recognized by St. Bernardo.[28]

Elevating the Laity

Arnold's opponents feared his ability to talk with, teach, preach to, and converse with common people. His rapport with the laity is acknowledged in one way or another by most witnesses; each writer has some such comment on Arnold's relations with lay people whether in Brescia, Paris, Zurich, or Rome.

Otto, reporting specifically about Arnold *in* Brescia, wrote, "[He was] a flatterer only of the laity. For he used to say that neither clerics that owned property, nor bishops that had regalia, nor monks with possessions could in any wise be saved. All these things belong to the prince, and should be bestowed of his beneficence for the use of the laity only."[29]

Whether Arnold went so far as to deny the possibility of salvation for the people Otto indicates, or whether Arnold's prophetic words were more on the order of Augustine's remark, "the clerk who gives up the monastic life is half lost," Arnold did not hesitate to convince people through his preaching and teaching that the wealth and power of the clergy were not of Christ nor for Christ's benefit. This made clergy who did not live by the tenets that Arnold espoused extremely uncomfortable and angry, but everybody knew Arnold lived what he taught to the fullest.

He rejected the church's claim of universal supremacy and the presumptions of the papacy. He did not accept the doctrine by which popes and bishops claimed that authority came from God first to the church in the person of the pope, by virtue of apostolic succession from Peter; that divine authority flowed from the Bishop of Rome down through the bishops and

---

28. Alfieri, *Story of Brescia*, 594.
29. Otto, *Deeds*, 143. John of Salisbury wrote about Arnold's appeal to lay people in Rome, including women. See Appendix I.A., 128.

clergy on the spiritual side of life, and through the emperor and kings on the temporal side. *Both* the spiritual and the temporal swords, they maintained, were entrusted to the church. God intended the church to wield the spiritual sword directly, and that secular rulers—kings and nobles wield the sword of governance at the *command of the church*. This view was expressed by Bernard of Clairvaux.[30]

Arnold's view was decisively different—the *people* have God-granted power. His experience among the people led him to believe that the movement for self-determination arising in the commune of Brescia and other cities in Lombardy and throughout Europe was healthful, an appropriate movement of the spirit that was logically commensurate with reform in the church.

The church's role, according to Arnold, is to minister by serving people and caring for their souls. In order to preach, teach, and minister, the church must disentangle itself from compromises inherent in wealth and power and from the double-mindedness of ulterior objectives. It is the role of the laity to nurture the earth and society so as to gain its bounty and blessing and to establish civic life. The laity is free for those enterprises and, for lay people, striving for gain and taking responsibility for affairs of state is not a compromise. To do this well requires government established by the people—who rightly pay their tithes.

Otto's choice of the word "flatterer" in describing Arnold implies he was a person engaged in manipulative seeking of favor and support. However, the Bergamese Poet wrote: "He condemned the laymen for not paying their tithes, and he condemned all taking of usury."[31] Would such talk feel like flattery to laypersons such as Brescian entrepreneurs? The Poet goes on to say, "Following Scripture, he taught that shameful greed, war, hatred, lust, perjury, murder, theft, deception, and the evil desires of the flesh are hindrances to eternal life." The term "flatterer" hardly seems appropriate to someone who preached like this. It would be more accurate to say this preacher flattered no one.

---

30. Bernard of Clairvaux, *De Consideratione*, 118.

31. The Bergamese Poet, *Frederick in Italy (Gesta di federico primi in Italia)*, 341. See also Appendix I.D., 137-139. The poetic Latin text can be found in *Carman de Gestis Federici I, Imperatoris in Lombardia*, 26-29. This poem about Frederick's campaign in Italy, discovered in the Vatican Library and published by E. Monaci in 1887, contains 100 lines about Arnold's life.

"He spared no vice, and like a foolish doctor, he cut away the healthy along with the diseased."[32] Such comments by Arnold's opponents charging him with an excess of righteous intolerance are common. It is difficult to assess to what extent these charges describe Arnold accurately. They are the most serious criticisms brought against him.

Nevertheless, Arnold's preaching, active ministry among people, and his exemplary life won him the respect of those among whom he lived. Thus, Map reports, "He went about preaching, 'seeking not the things which are his but those which are God's,' and he became loved and respected by all."[33]

Arnold was a leveler. His ideas made hierarchy tremble, especially later, when they were put into practice in Rome.

Teaching on the Sacraments of Baptism and Communion

There is no precise information on Arnold's teaching regarding the sacraments of baptism and communion, so we must again make an effort to construct some understanding of them and why he was attacked for them.

To begin, we have Otto's statement: "He is said to have held *unreasonable* [emphasis added] views with regard to the sacrament of the altar and infant baptism." Otto did not claim personal knowledge of Arnold's doctrines and acknowledged that he is passing along hearsay. He doesn't seem to know what those "unreasonable views" actually are, but apparently they *were different* and people talked about them.

Surely Arnold thought through the meaning of the sacraments carefully. He was, after all, a student of Peter Abelard and had studied *Sic et Non*. During his time in Brescia, he likely read Abelard's *Christian Theology* and his commentary on Romans as they became available. There can be little doubt that Arnold agreed with Augustine, Abelard, and most Christians that a sacrament is "a visible sign of invisible grace."[34]

Abelard described baptism as the Christian's marriage to God. Baptism, like marriage, is a kind of dedication like circumcision, which it replaces, and to which it is far superior, because it can be performed on both women and men, and because it cleanses the whole body, rather than focusing on only one part. Thus baptism makes good sense as a ritual of dedication. Water is the material of baptism and as it visibly cleanses the

---

32. Ibid.
33. Map, *Courtiers Trifles*, 50. See Appendix I.E., 140.
34. Sikes, *Abailard*, 212.

body it signifies the cleansing of the soul within.[35] However, for Abelard, *intention* was what mattered. In his view, baptism into the fellowship of salvation could be done *without* water. It could be done without knowing about the ritual or its story. That's a different view!

In his *Christian Theology*, Abelard refers to Ambrose on this matter.

> Ambrose writing to the sisters of the Emperor Valentinian at the time of the Emperor's death says: "I hear that you grieve because he did not receive the sacrament of baptism. Yet he had vowed that when he came to Italy he would be received into the church, and had signified his desire of being baptized by me. Has he not then the grace which he desired? Because he asked it, he has it."[36]

Resistance to Peter's, and, likely, Arnold's, teaching on baptism as marriage to God, arose in large part because it departed in emphasis from Augustine's. Augustine and Abelard had different visions of salvation. Augustine looked *back* to the sin of Eve and Adam—the "original sin" of humans with its burden of guilt. Thus, baptism was *required* in order to *cancel* the guilt of original sin. Salvation through baptism delivered one from the burden of guilt by providing a way for humans to participate in the sacrificial death of Christ on the cross and rise again with him, cleansed of sin.

Abelard, on the other hand, looked *forward* toward fulfillment in actual human living through the salvific nature of love. He wrote: "The revelation of the Cross was that of divine love inciting to responsive love in conduct of life."[37] Augustine's teaching was prevalent at the time and regarded as basic; it had been confirmed at the Council of Carthage in 418. The teachings of Peter and Arnold, according to the widely accepted view of things—the conventional wisdom—were frivolous and dangerous. Bernard and others wanted to leave things well enough alone; they directly attacked the teachings of Arnold and Peter Abelard in the thirties and forties as we shall see.

Peter held that a person is *not* guilty by heredity—surely a shocking assertion to Bernard and contrary to the mainstream of accepted doctrine. Although humans are prone to evil, ignorance, and weakness, they are not sinful just by being alive. *Consent* to evil or wrong causes sin. "Thus a transgressor is not one who does what is prohibited. He is one who consents to what is prohibited."[38] McCallum comments: "The clue to what is sin lies,

35. Ibid., 214.
36. Abelard, *Christian Theology*, 65, 66.
37. Ibid., 103.
38. Abelard, *Ethics or Know Thyself*, 30.

therefore, in personal intention, and not in the guilty nature of man."[39] Abelard thought good intention brought about by the Holy Spirit may be sufficient for salvation. What then is the role of baptism? Does everyone need it? Does everyone need the church? Abelard, even more readily than Dante, believed pagans, though unbaptized by water and without Christian ceremony, could be saved and that some, for sure, were.[40]

Abelard had put the matter of the relation of baptism to salvation in front of himself and his students in Contradictions 106–116 of *Sic et Non*. Contradiction 106 states the issue directly, "That without the baptism of water no one can be saved, and the contrary."[41] Later, Abelard advocated that baptism's purpose is to *draw* the person forward by the *example* of Christ. He quoted the insight of Horace: "Good men hate to sin from love of virtue" and added, "[Horace] implies that love of virtue is better than fear of punishment as a deterrent from vice."[42] This reflects confidence in positive reinforcement and trust in the strength and effectiveness of love—especially, divine love.

Some Baptist theologians claim that Arnold replaced infant baptism with "believer's baptism." This seems unlikely. If either Abelard or Arnold advocated discontinuing infant baptism, it could hardly have gone unmentioned. Calling for penitence on the part of the parents and sponsors, however, is a proper, conscious act that intends good for the future of this child. The people who care for this little one profess that they will try to be on their best behavior.

Neither Arnold nor Peter abandoned the practice of baptism; there is not a shred of evidence to support that. Baptisms have almost always been times of joy. Clergy enjoy baptizing people; it's hard to find a better part of the job. Especially so if you are Arnold, and you believe baptism blesses for the future giving all the more cause for joy. However, theologians looking on from a distance without participating existentially, limiting their views to theory and theology, might think these convictions strange.

Following Peter, Arnold likely thought unbaptized persons could be saved. If so, he, too, opposed Augustine by admitting the possibility of salvation outside the church. In his prophetic preaching he would have had occasion to quote: "God is able from these stones to raise up children of

---

39. McCallum, *Christian Theology*, 101.
40. Abelard, Ibid., 66.
41. McCallum, Ibid., 103.
42. Abelard, Ibid., 61.

Abraham" (Luke 3:8) and also Jesus' prophecy about the judgment of "all the nations." "Come, you that are blessed by my Father, inherit the kingdom prepared for you from the foundation of the world; for I was hungry and you gave me food, I was thirsty and you gave me something to drink, I was a stranger and you welcomed me, I was naked and you gave me clothing, I was sick and you took care of me, I was in prison and you visited me." The "sheep" of the story asked *when* had they done so. Jesus answered: "Truly I tell you, just as you did it to one of the least of these who are members of my family, you did it to me" (Matt. 25).

Peter Abelard's view of communion, and likely by extension Arnold's, is less clear. Unfortunately, the parts of Abelard's *Introduction to Theology* that contain most of his teaching on the sacraments are lost.[43] However, in contradictions 117 and 118 of *Sic et Non* he included discussion of the later Protestant doctrine that became known as "consubstantiation"—that Christ is *present* in the elements, alongside the prevailing view known as "transubstantiation" in which the bread and wine *become* the body and blood of Jesus.

This does not tell us much about why Arnold's teaching about communion was thought "unreasonable" according to Otto of Friesing. Reasons that come to mind are that Arnold entertained a view close to "consubstantiation" or possibly because of variances in practice such as, for example, frequency of communion.

The emphasis upon intention raised the specter of Pelagianism. Pelagius (354–420) asserted free will in opposition to the doctrine of predestination. He taught that original sin did not taint human nature, and that people can choose good or evil without special divine assistance. After years of controversy, Pelagius had been condemned a heretic at the Council of Carthage in 418, and Pelagianism was one of the charges brought against Peter Abelard at Sens (1141) for which he, too, was declared a heretic. At the Council of Sens, which we will discuss in chapter 4, Arnold was condemned along with Peter, a strong indication that Arnold held similar views.

Summary

The commune of Brescia was enriched by the presence of the canons of San Pietro and the teaching and preaching of Arnold. His teaching about temporal power encouraged revolution and ultimately brought about his exile. Although he may have advanced this conviction from the first, at

---

43. Sikes, *Abailard*, 214.

some point between 1135 and 1138 he took a stand with the commune against his bishop. Bishop Manfred brought the matter to the pope, who, on Manfred's second try, responded in his bishop's favor. As Alfieri puts it:

> We don't know the particular sites of this struggle, but we know well its epilogue: the consuls were expelled and Arnold was accused by bishop Manfredo of being a disturber of the peace.
>
> In Rome, Innocent II received the bishop's complaints, but he limited himself to forbidding Arnold to preach and ordered him to leave Italy (note: Italy) and to not return without his authorization. The relative mildness of this measure proves that Arnold wasn't judged to be either a heretic or a sower of scandal and schism, but, at the most, a *patarin* whose activities were untimely at that moment, but not truly dangerous, nor, for that matter, worthy of heavy condemnation. And take note that Rome was extremely vigilant.[44]

It came about that Arnold, Austin canon regular and abbot of San Pietro, after nineteen years of Christian service in his home town, left Brescia to continue his vocation elsewhere.

---

44. Alfieri, *Story of Brescia*, 594.

4

On the Move

It would help if we had some information—some words from the silent (to us) reformer, prophet, and democratic visionary, Arnold—about how he felt, what he said, what courses of action he considered, and how he decided to go to Paris after he received news of his exile.

How did he receive the news? Was it a letter from the pope? A letter from Bishop Manfred? A visit from Bishop Manfred? A public announcement by the Prefecture in the Plaza Duomo, the main square of Brescia? Did he learn by being arrested by officers of the bishop? Or, by officers of the commune who had, for the time being, become compliant with ecclesiastical authority? Was his community at San Pietro instructed to exile him? Did he receive word by letter or mouth from Peter Abelard inviting him to Mont-Sainte-Geneviève?

Was Arnold angry? What did he say in his last sermon? Did he preach to the people of Brescia as well as to his brother canons?

Our task is to trail our man who was becoming an apostle of liberty. Our scenario must be probable and our scenario must respect the texts. We know that Arnold left Brescia and became a colleague of Peter Abelard. Trailing him will take a bit of digging.

Between Brescia and Paris

We are faced at the outset with the task of trying to determine and date Arnold's activity as he moved from Brescia to Paris. John of Salisbury tells us, that while Manfred "was absent on a short visit to Rome" in 1138, Abbot

Arnold of Brescia, Apostle of Liberty

Arnold "so swayed the minds of the citizens that they would scarcely open their gates to the bishop on his return."[1] According to Greenaway, Bishop Manfred had gone to Rome to get help against the rebellious commune, an act that may have provoked Arnold into action.[2] In any event, he stepped forward and proclaimed his opposition to episcopal rule and his support for the commune.[3]

Manfred's initial appeal was unsuccessful because Innocent was preoccupied with the papal schism. Conflicts were abundant. Popes and want-to-be popes had their hands full. A lot was happening in this medieval twelfth-century world. Upon his return to Brescia, Manfred was scarcely able to enter the city. A year later, Manfred returned to Rome for the Second Lateran Council, convened on April 4, 1139. After the council, Innocent gave Manfred the judgment he wanted.[4]

So, Arnold left Brescia in the spring or early summer of 1139 and traveled from place to place as he made his way out of Italy—a journey that contrasts with travel by air or on super highways in which the traveler by passes most places and towns. His choices were to head west across Lombardy to Helvetia, Burgundy, and France, or north toward Germany. He chose intellectual action in Paris, where he could teach and study with Abelard. The community at San Pietro might have participated in this decision. Arnold may have experienced his exile from Brescia as a release and an opportunity for a fresh start. In any event, he headed to Paris to take up a teaching ministry.

The Bergamese Poet reported that, "He also stirred up great Milan."[5] Milan was on Arnold's way as he crossed Italy. In a prophetic voice he called the church and the papacy to the further reform of shedding temporal power and using wealth to *benefit the poor*. His message was received enthusiastically by the people of Milan who had previously responded to the Milanese reformer, Arialdus, martyred in 1065 and later canonized. Arialdus had preached virtually the same reform agenda as did Arnold.

At the time of Arnold's visit in 1139, Milan, with its tradition of independence, was not inclined to look to papal Rome for authority. Ambrose, a

---

1. John of Salisbury, *Historia Pontificalis*, 63. See Appendix I.A. From John we learn that Arnold went to Paris to join Abelard. His presence provided added fuel for Bernard's invectives against Abelard (Letter 239, Appendix I.C., 132, 133).

2. Greenaway, *Arnold.*, 51.

3. Ibid.

4. Ibid., 56.

5. The Bergamese Poet, *Frederick in Italy*, 341. See Appendix I.D., 138.

On the Move

great and true spiritual descendent of Peter and Paul and the other apostles, was Milan's spiritual father and by him, through their church, the Milanese had spawned the great Augustine as well. They did not think themselves second to anyone and they often opposed papal power. Prior to 1122, Milan had looked to German kings rather than to popes for investiture. Its reform impetus, similar to Brescia, arose from the *patarin* and was, therefore, civic as well as ecclesiastical. Earlier, reform had been channeled by the work of the great papal legate, Peter Damian, who calmed and directed Milan in 1059 and the years following, in support of the papacy. But, Milan's alliance with the papacy was intermittent.

During the eleventh century reform, the commune had considered the papacy an appropriate check against the power and abuses of its own bishops. Reform directed against simony and lay investiture had popular support. Arnold's preaching in 1139 must have seemed the next logical step of reform, because abusive wealth and the exercise of secular power by the church and clergy persisted.

The former abbot of San Pietro could not stay in Milan—he had been banished from Italy. Leaving Milan, he could have followed the same route he had taken as a prospective student on his way to Paris, passing under the Arch of Augustus in Aosta, climbing the Alps through Great St. Bernard Pass, descending to Lake Geneva, and heading on to Paris.

His arrival in Paris must have been anticipated. Canons and students arriving from Italy surely brought news of Arnold of Brescia and his exile. This was not done in secret; it was big news. Stories of a canon who espoused scholarship, entertained bold ideas, and fearlessly preached separation of the church from wealth and secular power were just the thing to catch the interest of students. As it became known to Abelard's students that Arnold would be joining the faculty, so to speak, interest heightened.

Arnold entered the circle of his famous former master, Peter Abelard, at the Augustinian house of Mont-Sainte-Geneviève in the parish of Saint Hilary. We suspect he took residence in Mont-Sainte-Geneviève rather than St. Victor, another house of canons nearby. Its abbot, Hugh of St. Victor (c. 1096–1141), had established high standards of scholarship, which included staying current with Abelard's thinking: "[T]he group of thinkers [known as Victorines] who were in the house [St. Victor] between the 1120s and the 1160s undertook patiently to censor, amend, absorb and surpass Abelard's theological production. A readiness to censure defects was graced with a striving to provide alternative theses by means of a scholarship which rivaled that of Abelard himself."⁶

Soon' dealing with Bernard of Clairvaux became front and center. As a cadre of divines attacked Peter, Hyacinth and Arnold stepped into the breech. "[Arnold] . . . together with Master Hyacinth, who is now a cardinal, zealously fostered his cause against the abbot of Clairvaux."⁷ Surely the affair invigorated the entire school. Arnold had plenty to do—teaching, duties as a canon, and keeping up with developments. Arnold, Peter, and Hyacinth must have conversed intensely and often, research was needed and letters, pamphlets, and papers written. Adrenalin flowed and life had zest.

The Council of Sens—Story of a Rigged Trial

Arnold's concerns included intellectual and theological issues as well as social and political reform. Peter Abelard, though clearly sympathetic to democratic civic life,⁸ and no doubt able to offer brilliant insights regarding church practice, organization, and ministry, had his mind mainly on theological spade work, seeking greater understanding of life and faith. However, his willingness to challenge authority struck fear in the heart of the established order, and bringing Arnold into the mix exacerbated that fear.

The citizens of Reims, for example, were intent on forming a commune. The situation went from violence to settlement and back to violence. During the later thirties the attitude toward communes hardened among church leaders and royalty. Good conservative, Christian leaders feared upheaval of the social structure. To them, Abelard's challenge to theological authority was of one cloth with rebellion among the masses. There was more at stake in the battle with Abelard than theology.

Constant Mews set about to explore this seldom studied aspect of the establishment's fear of social upheaval.

> The confrontation between the two men at Sens has often been interpreted as a clash between innovation and tradition, the questioning culture of the schools confronting an older, monastic way of thinking, characterized by respect for religious authority and monastic tradition. Yet does this really explain the intensity of Bernard's rhetoric about the threat presented to the church by

---

6. Luscombe, *School*, 183, 184.

7. John of Salisbury, *Historia Pontificalis*, 63 and Appendix I.A., 128.

8. Abelard, *Christian Theology*, 63.

Peter Abelard and his "shield bearer," Arnold of Brescia? Why did Bernard of Clairvaux evoke such apocalyptic language to describe the threat presented by the unlikely alliance of a teacher with a preacher normally identified with the Italian communes rather than with the schools of Paris?[9]

There is more to it, thinks Mews, much more. Bernard and fellow clergy feared wild, speculative ideas about God and Christian doctrine, believing they fueled opposition to authority in general. At the very moment they were fighting a commune that was trying to overthrow episcopal government in Reims,[10] and facing threats of same in other cities, here came Arnold of Brescia, a known Italian revolutionary, a preacher who supported communes and had been exiled for his actions. They must have thought that by taking Arnold in, Abelard demonstrated for the pope, clergy, and kings the destructive impact of the reckless pursuits of liberal schools. Danger was heightened, thought the protectors of the social order, by the knowledge that there were many, even in the curia, who entertained such ideas and eagerly read the writings of Peter Abelard.

Although Peter and Arnold's students likely supported a new sociopolitical order emphasized by the presence of Master Arnold, theological ideas and theological method were still of primary interest and concern. While many churchmen disliked the very idea of such bold exploration, attractive, brilliant Peter paid no heed. Students loved him, a fact difficult to contend with. Now, Arnold of Brescia was in the mix. A council was needed to provide a proper setting for the anticipated showdown.

The story of the Council of Sens, insofar as it was a confrontation between Abelard and Bernard, begins with Abelard's book, *Theologia*, falling by chance into the hands of Abbot William of St. Thierry (C. 1075–1148), near Reims. During Lent of 1140,[11] he wrote to Bernard and Bishop Geoffrey of Chartres, a papal legate, who had been a defender of Peter at Soisson in 1121.[12]

---

9. Mews, "The Council of Sens," 344.

10. Ibid., 351. "Even in November 1140, Reims was still divided between supporters and opponents of the commune."

11. Ibid., 381, 382. There has been much discussion as to whether Sens occurred in 1140 or 1141, 1140 previously most widely accepted. Mews makes a persuasive case for May 25, 1141, which means that William's letter was written during Lent of 1140.

12. Greenaway, *Arnold*, 66, n. 3. It appears Geoffrey made no response to William's letter of alarm. He was, however, one of the signers of the letter written by the bishops of France to Innocent after the Council of Sens asking the pope to condemn Abelard.

> For Peter Abaelard is again teaching and publishing novelties; his books cross the seas, pass over the Alps; new speculations concerning the doctrines of the Faith, and new dogmas are spread throughout provinces and realms, are openly preached and freely defended; it is even said that they have partisans in the Curia in Rome. I say to you that your silence is dangerous, as well as for your selves as for the Church of God. . . . [He] makes himself a critic of the Faith and not a disciple; an improver of it, instead of a follower.[13]

William's letter to Bernard was accompanied by his rebuttal—*Disputation adversus Abaelardus*. In it he took issue with Peter Abelard's thoughts on the Trinity, the atonement, the Eucharist, and original sin. As he saw it, Peter had become a critic of the faith by applying dialectics to theology.[14] The abbot of Clairvaux responded to William:

> To his dear friend William, from Brother Bernard.

> In my opinion your misgivings are well called-for and reasonable. This is evident from your booklet in which you bruise and close "the lips that mutter wickedness". Not that I have yet had the opportunity to read it with the attention you require but, from what I have been able to see by glancing through it, I like it very much and consider it well able to overthrow the iniquitous teaching. As you well know, I am not in the habit of trusting much my judgement, especially in such grave matters as these, so I suggest that it would be worth our while to meet somewhere, as soon as we have an opportunity, and discuss the whole thing. But I do not think this can be arranged before Easter, lest we are distracted from the prayer that is proper to this season of Lent. I beg you in the meantime, to suffer patiently my own patience and silence, for at present I know little or nothing at all of these matters. Yet in answer to your prayers God can give me the power for what you are urging me to do. Farewell.[15]

Subsequently, Bishop Stephen of Paris invited Bernard to the city to preach. Bernard encouraged Peter's students to repudiate their teacher's

---

13. William of St. Thierry, Letter, 852, 853 in *The Life and Works of Saint Bernard*, Vol. II.

14. Secondary accounts of the events of the Council of Sens include Mews, "Council," Sikes, *Abailard*, 219-247, Murray, *Abelard and St Bernard*, especially pages 35 ff., and Luscombe, *School*, especially pages 103-142.

15. Bernard of Clairvaux, *Letters*, 236:314, 315.

books and to turn from the Babylon of student life in Paris to the Jerusalem of monasticism.[16] Bernard met personally with Abelard twice prior to Sens intentionally following the direction of Scripture (Matthew 18:15–17) for dealing with an erring brother. Abelard, as Bernard likely expected, did not budge.[17]

Bernard's sermon, *"de Conversione ad Clericos"* (Conversion of the Clergy), aimed at converting students to the monastic life; that is what he meant by conversion. In the sermon as we have it, he did not directly attack Abelard; he stressed the hazards of city and student life in contrast to monastic life. "Flee from the midst of Babylon. Flee and save your souls. Flock to the city of refuge."[18] As with his meetings with Abelard, Bernard had limited success with the students—although Geoffrey of Auxerre, author of *Bernard, Vita Prima*, until then a disciple of Abelard, was converted to Bernard's side by this sermon.[19]

It was no surprise that Abelard and his students thought the abbot's remarks were directed against them. Taking exception to Bernard's approach to theology and his attack on Master Peter, the students urged a public debate. Believing Bishop Stephen of Paris to be hostile to Abelard (it was Stephen who had invited Bernard to Paris to preach and recruit monks) the students took advantage of an absence of Stephen from Paris to request Henry Sanglier (ca. 1085–1142) Archbishop of Sens, the metropolitan of the province, to provide a forum.[20]

Once plans for a contest were in motion, the passionate and energetic students of Abelard became increasingly eager for the debate. They were confident; who could defeat Peter Abelard—the *"Rhinoceros Indomitus,"* "the Socrates of Gaul?"

Henry was not eager to host this debate. Independent of this issue and before receiving this request, he had called for a gathering of his bishops to

---

16. Evidence for these activities is found in the biography of Bernard by his contemporary, Geoffrey of Auxerre—*Bernard, Vita Prima*, and in the account of the Council, written by Bernard and signed by the Bishops of France. Mabillon Editor, *Bernard Works*, Letter CLXXXVII:868.

17. Sikes, 226, 227. Sikes speculates Bernard became aware of Arnold's presence during these visits.

18. Bernard of Clairvaux, *Sermons on Conversion*, 75.

19. Luscombe, *School*, 50.

20. Sikes, *Abailard*, 228. This information is found in a letter by Abelard discovered relatively recently. The letter has been published in *Medieval and Renaissance Studies*, 5 (1961), 1–28 by Raymond Klibansky, "Peter Abailard and Bernard of Clairvaux", 6, 7.

showcase newly acquired relics and the great new church he was building in Sens. He even invited King Louis VII. The event "was to be a show of national unity before the relics of St. Stephen, as well as an occasion to assert the dignity of the archbishopric of Sens over its suffragan dioceses, including both Chartres and Paris."[21] And, while no fan of Peter Abelard, Henry had a strained relationship with Bernard, enhancing his reluctance.

As Henry explained to the pope, he called a council at Peter's request only after repeated demands.

> [Bernard] encouraged many of the students to renounce and reject books full of poison and to fear and abstain from teaching that harmed catholic faith. Master Peter, suffering this less than patiently and too bitterly, frequently began to harass us, and did not wish to stop doing so, until we wrote to the lord abbot of Clairvaux and instructed him to come to into our presence on the assigned day, namely the octave of Pentecost at Sens, where Master Peter described and presented himself as ready to justify and defend the teaching which the abbot of Clairvaux had criticized, as has been explained.[22]

It is ironic that the confrontation with Bernard was arranged through the initiative of Abelard and his students, unlike the Council of Soissons to which he was summoned. As we will see, it's difficult to imagine things working out better strategically for Bernard. Perhaps he laid a trap and Peter fell into it.

What was Arnold's role? Was he the lead colleague, as his eventual co-condemnation at Sens suggests? Did he work behind the scenes among the students? John of Salisbury said Peter Abelard's closest supporters were Arnold and Hyacinth Boboni. The two of them, he wrote: "zealously fostered his cause against the abbot of Clairvaux."[23] Other major figures were present or in contact with Abelard during this time. In addition to Hyacinth Boboni, we know of Guy of Castello, Gilbert de la Porrée, and Berengar of Poitiers. The first three were well known; two of of them became pope.

Hyacinth Boboni (1106–1198) was a member of the papal court. His signature is found on papal documents beginning in 1121, he became a subdeacon in 1126, a cardinal in 1144, and was elected Pope Celestine III in 1191. John of Salisbury reported his presence at Sens and Bernard

---

21. Mews, *Council*, 355.
22. Archbishop Henry, *The Works*, Mabillon, 869.
23. John of Salisbury, *Historia Pontificalis*, 63. Appendix I.A., 128.

complained of Hyacinth's "ill will" toward himself in letters to Pope Innocent and Cardinal Haimeric.[24]

Master Guy of Castello (d. 1144), cardinal priest of St. Mark, though probably not at Sens, was in Paris for several months in 1139-40 and, it seems clear, spent time with Abelard, Arnold, and the group of students and scholars who surrounded them. Bernard wrote Guy after the council urging him not to love the errors of one he loves, meaning of course, Peter Abelard. "Such love is earthy, animal, diabolical, and harmful," Bernard wrote.[25] Guy became Pope Celestine II in 1143. "Guy is the only associate of Abelard, except for Heloise, who is known to have possessed copies of Abelard's writings."[26]

Gilbert de la Porrée (c. 1070-1154) was renowned as a brilliant scholar and friend of Peter's. He taught at the cathedral school of Chartres prior to his election as bishop of Poitiers in 1142. In 1148 he, too, was brought to trial by Bernard, this time at the Council of Reims. Both Otto of Freising and John of Salisbury give accounts of that trial.[27]

Berengar of Poitiers (1110-1188), a defender of Abelard, wrote a satirical account of the Council of Sens called *Apologeticus*. Vigorous and perhaps extreme, it provided an alternative account of the Council. Other than his authorship of two other documents, very little is known of Berengar's life. Luscombe provides a summary of Berengar's *Apologeticus* with comments.[28]

From the time the date of the challenge was set until the council convened, Arnold must have been busy. Archbishop Henry had acceded to Peter's request and the debate was set for the Cathedral of Sens. Extensive discussions about relevant matters ranging from the theological points at issue to the politics of the situation were necessary and surely consumed many hours for Peter, Arnold, Hyacinth, and others.[29] Their energy was fueled by errors in Bernard's charges, his misunderstanding of several of

---

24. Bernard, *Letters*, 328:239, 249.
25. Ibid., 320:249
26. Luscombe, *School*, 21.
27. Otto, *Deeds*, 82 and 88f. John of Salisbury, *Historia Pontificalis*, 17f.
28. Luscombe, *School*, 29-49.
29. At this time, Peter was 61, Arnold 40, Hyacinth 34, Berengar 30, Bernard 50, and Gilbert in his 60s. We do not know Guy of Castello's birth year so we do not know his age. *The Catholic Enclyclopedia* reports that he was an elderly man when he became pope in 1143.

Peter's assertions, *and* for saying that his *Theologia* should be called *Stultilogia* (stupidology or fool-teaching).[30]

Peter, not yet knowing Bernard's response to Henry, wrote to friends and students—his "comrades," urging them to be present. He expressed his opinion of the man bringing charges against him. "Certainly that man, for a long time now a secret enemy, who has pretended until this point to be a friend, even the greatest of friends, has now blazed out into such great envy that he could not bear the fame of my writings, by which he believed his glory to be debased the more as he thought that I was elevated the more."[31]

The students probably spent much time discussing these matters in the bistros of Paris, fanning flames of anticipation, anxious to see their man, their leader, put the—from their point of view—presumptuous, pious-mouthed Bernard in his place, likely adding more adjectives and names that have not been passed along.

Beyond particular theological issues, intellectual honesty and the freedom to use critical method, such as outlined in the introduction of *Sic et Non,* were at stake. Peter, Arnold, and their students saw themselves pursuing and defending the God-given faculty of reason against the authoritarianism of Bernard and his allies. They did not think of themselves as heretics or sponsors of heretics, far from it. Peter and Arnold were as concerned to combat heresy as Bernard. Sikes observes:

> In fact, Abelard was convinced that use of reason was vital for effectively combating heresy. He was, we must remember, engaged in the training of students who might perhaps have to withstand the teaching of these unorthodox professors, and he therefore considered it important that his students should be able to understand the reasons by which their own beliefs could be defended. Living at a time when so much heresy existed, when new sects were springing up in the south of France, it was the duty of professors and students alike to train themselves in such a way as would enable them to convince the heretic of his errors.[32]

Bernard, for his part, objected to the liberties Abelard took, whether resulting in heresy or not. He wrote Cardinal Ivo:

> He oversteps the landmarks placed by our Fathers in discussing and writing about faith, the sacraments and the Holy Trinity; he

---

30. Ziolkowski, ed. *Letters of Peter Abelard,* 102 and 109, n. 24.
31. Abelard, Ibid., 108.
32. Sikes, *Abailard,* 249, 250.

changes each thing according to his pleasure, adding to it or taking from it. He is a man who does not know his limitations making void the virtue of the cross by the cleverness of his words. Nothing in heaven or on earth is hidden from him, except himself.[33]

In this connection it is worth noting that Peter had written to Bernard years earlier, after Bernard had called upon Heloise and the sisters at the Paraclete (ca. 1131). Bernard criticized the version of the Lord's prayer Heloise and her sisters were using as instructed by Peter. The sisters were praying "give us this day our supersubstantial bread" meaning spiritual bread (from the Gospel of Matthew), while Bernard claimed that the accepted way was "give us this day our daily bread" (from the Gospel of Luke). The letter is impressive and the arguments learned.

Indicating that Bernard was a slave to custom and ignored truth, Peter wrote: "Whoever he be let him notice that *use* [emphasis added] is not to be preferred to reason nor custom to truth." In the letter, Peter quoted Gregory VII: [W]hat the Lord says should be pointed out: 'I am,' he said, 'the truth'; he did not say, 'I am custom.'"[34] There is no evidence of a response to this letter from Bernard; clearly, these two had a history.

Upon receiving Archbishop Henry's letter requesting his presence at Sens, Bernard protested that he was no match for a debater such as Peter Abelard. He wrote to Pope Innocent, "[W]hen all have fled before him, he calls me out, the least of all, to single combat. . . . I refused because I am but a child in this sort of warfare and he is a man habituated to it from his youth, and because I deemed it an unworthy action to bring the faith into the arena of controversy, resting as it does on sure and immutable truth."[35] Nevertheless, the abbot "sorrowfully" bowed to the advice of friends who said that Abelard's errors "might appear to be confirmed if there were no one to answer and refute them."[36]

Should we take Bernard at face value when he proclaimed his inexperience and weakness? These words might be tournament tactics—his method of approaching a contest. Bernard was a formidable contestant. Whether he was being modest, vying for position, or genuinely fearful about this event, his experience campaigning for Pope Innocent II against the antipope, and

---

33. Bernard, *Letters*, 241:321. This letter, written after the Council of Sens, reflects accurately Bernard's stance throughout.
34. Abelard, Letter Ten, Ziolkowsky, 85–98.
35. Bernard, *Letters*, 239:318.
36. Ibid., 319.

the reputation, confidence, and charisma he had when he went into action, were much more than needed to defeat Abelard, as Bernard's friends such as William of St. Thierry, confidently expected.

The abbot left nothing to chance. He wrote the bishops of the Archdiocese of Sens summoning them to the "fight," making it clear that they must be there. He called in his chips, so to speak. "Even if it were only in defence of himself [referring to himself], your child might, perhaps not unreasonably, pride himself on your protection. But now because it is your affair, nay, more yours than mine, I advise and earnestly beg you to prove yourselves friends in adversity."[37]

Bernard's success and reputation were due to more than inspiration and charisma. He wrote volumes of letters and followed up on many matters, reprimanding, praising, and requesting favors for friends. He was loyal and faithful to friends and supporters. This paid dividends.

When it came to the council itself, Bernard proved himself the master. He arranged a meeting of the bishops to play the "jury" the night before the opening of the council. He had a lector read extracts from Peter's works and then went on to "prove" them heretical. In his *Apologeticus*, Berengar of Poitiers, Peter's friend in attendance, described this meeting as an after-dinner drinking bout. While the lector read, the rest of the prelates drank until they became sleepy. Then the lector stopped the reading and put to the nearly deaf ears of the bishops the question: *"Damnatis?"* (Do you damn this?) The priests could scarcely respond their affirmation "namus" (We swim).[38] Berengar satirically compared Bernard's gathering to the council of the Pharisees in the Gospel of John.

> The chief priests and the Pharisees gathered a council and said: What do we, for this man doth many miracles? If we let him alone so, all will believe in him. But one of them, named Bernard the abbot, being the high priest of that council, prophesied, saying: It is expedient for us that one man should be exterminated by the people that the whole nation perish not. From that day therefore they devised to have him condemned.[39]

The letter of the bishops to Innocent summarizing the council acknowledged this prior meeting.

---

37. Ibid., 237:315.

38. Luscombe, *School*, 32. In footnote 4 on pages 29 and 30, Luscombe provides bibliographic information on *Apologeticus*.

39. Berengar, *Apologeticus*, Ibid.

But as to his errors in doctrine, which had infected many, and had penetrated into the deepest recesses of not a few hearts, we had condemned them the day before Abaelard made his appeal, after having heard them plainly and undoubtedly proved to be heretical, both by convincing reasonings and by authorities cited from S. Augustine and other Fathers by the Abbot of Clairvaux.[40]

Bernard used virtually the same tactic again seven years later at the Council of Reims (1148). Before publicly engaging Gilbert de la Porrée, his target on that occasion, Bernard invited "all the leading churchmen, those who were distinguished by their learning or sanctity or office, to meet him privately in his lodging." He pressed them to affirm certain doctrines for condemning Gilbert. Led by Robert de Bosco, the prelates objected to Bernard's method and also to the fact that the pope and the cardinals were not present. Following Robert's lead, the meeting broke up.[41]

Some who had been present reported this meeting to the cardinals, who

> . . . were very wrath with the abbot and those who had assembled at his request: They agreed among themselves to support the cause of the bishop of Poitiers, *saying that the abbot had attacked master Peter in exactly the same way* [emphasis added]; but he [Abelard] had not had access to the apostolic see, which was accustomed to confound schemes of this kind and snatch the weak from the clutches of the strong.[42]

As John of Salisbury indicated, at the Council of Sens there was no one of sufficient power to protect master Peter. What happened at the Reims was a good example of the value of the papacy when functioning at its everyday best. It provided a court of appeal for the weak and for those overpowered by local powers. John's comment reveals that this papal role was considered beneficial. Used properly, it was appropriate; temporal power and the power of wealth were the inappropriate powers.

As has been mentioned several times, how one should *approach* theology was of great significance. Peter and Arnold drew from the ancient philosophers and the Latin classics to the consternation of the conservatives. The collegiality of the two men implies a large measure of agreement.

---

40. The Bishops' Letter to Pope Innocent reporting on the Council of Sens, Mabillon, 870, 871.

41. John of Salisbury, *Historia Pontificalis*, 17–21.

42. Ibid., 19, 20.

They may have had differences, but they were linked by their opponents, as Mews shows, with respect to the vital, though less explicit sociopolitical issue of communes.

The Council of Sens opened on Monday with Bernard reading the charges against Master Peter.[43] After the reading, Abelard surprised the gathering by refusing to answer; instead, he appealed to Rome. The report in the Bishops' Letter to the pope is as follows:

> In the presence, then, of the glorious King of France, Louis, of the pious, William, Count of Nevers, of the lord Archbishop of Reims with certain of his suffragans, except those of Paris and Nevers, of a great number of Abbots as pious as wise, and Magister Peter, with his supporters, respectively appeared. To speak briefly, the lord Abbot brought before us the book *Theologia*, written by Magister Peter, and pointed out from this book various propositions, which he stigmatized as absurd, or even plainly heretical, in order that Magister Peter might either deny that he had written them, or, if he accepted the authorship, might either justify or correct them. But Magister Peter appeared to be at a loss what to do; and, in order to make a way of escape, refused to reply, although he had a free hearing given to him, a safe place, and impartial judges; but appealing to your hearing in person, most holy Father, he left the assembly with all his supporters.[44]

However, Peter was *not* unprepared. In a letter addressed to Bernard but distributed more widely called the "Apologia Against Bernard of Clairvaux,"[45] Abelard responded to each of nineteen charges. He observed that some of the charges were made against things he had *not* written. With respect to others, he clarified his meaning and claimed Catholicity. Most scholars agree that he wrote this letter prior to Sens; the "Apologia" is astute and interesting; it demonstrates that Peter was prepared.

Perhaps knowing Peter was well prepared explains why Geoffrey of Auxerre, by then firmly attached to Bernard, considered Abelard's decision

---

43. Fourteen alleged errors were read under the title *Capitula Haeresum Petri Abelard*. They can be found in Mabillon, 556–564, preceeding Bernard's letter CXC. It is thought that the *Capitula* originally accompanied the Bishops' Letter to Pope Innocent. Epistle CXC (Mabillon, 565–591), *Contra quaedam Capitula errorum Abaelardi*, a letter from Bernard to Innocent, lists twenty-six errors under nine headings. There is an excellent discussion of the particular issues, including texts of the alleged errors and relevant selections from Abelard's writings, in Murray, 49–158.

44. The Bishops' Letter, Mabillon, 870.

45. Abelard, "Apologia," Ziolkowski, 111–129.

not to defend himself a miracle. Poole, however, thought Peter's action was the result of a character flaw. "But hardly had the council opened, hardly was the recital of his heresies begun, when, by a sudden revulsion of feeling, a failure of courage or a flash of certainty that the votes of the council were already secured—perhaps that the excited populace would rise against him—he appealed" to papal Rome.[46] These hypotheses are not necessary to explain Peter's action. Nor is Poole's assumption that the populace was *against* Abelard certain.

By meeting time of the morning assembly, it was unlikely Peter was unaware of the previous night's meeting. He could see how matters were stacked. This was not going to be a debate. Bishops and rulers under the power of Bernard, rather than bright, enthusiastic students and visionaries such as Arnold, or even Hyacinth, a member of the curia, would decide this matter. Clearly the decision had been made. The best he could do was appeal to Rome with its reputation for impartiality and a place where he had friends. He had expected a forum for discussion and had anticipated the exhilaration of a public debate about important theological matters. Instead, it was about his personal faith and charges to which he was required to respond with either yes or no. He was very disappointed.

Before the session opened, Peter probably gathered supporters to talk things through. Hyacinth, familiar with the people and procedures at the papacy, may have supported, even suggested, an appeal to the pope, seeing it a better chance than Sens allowed. Hindsight does not convince one that any other action could have gotten Peter out of the situation.

Otto of Freising: "While his [Abelard's] faith was being discussed there [Sens], fearing an uprising of the people, he asked that he might appear before the Roman see."[47] Assuming Otto's remark has substance, to what sort of uprising does he refer? In spite of Poole's interpretation above, is it likely the threat of violence by the people would be *against* Peter? Might it not as likely have been fear of a commune-type uprising? This was a high visibility event, the people of Sens would have been aware of the sociopolitical implications and of the presence of Arnold of Brescia, a popular hero, standing with Peter Abelard. If this were the case, Peter and Arnold did their opponents a favor in not forcing the issue.

Greenaway assumes that Peter made his decision to appeal to the pope without the support of Arnold. "He can hardly have been in Abelard's full

---

46. Poole, *Illustrations*, 164, 165.
47. Otto of Freising, *Deeds*, 84.

confidence, for he would certainly never have countenanced the appeal to Rome."[48] Not necessarily, not even likely. Neither the assertion that Arnold *was not* in Peter's full confidence nor that Arnold opposed *all* appeals to Rome stands on solid ground.

Peter set out for Cluny on his way to Rome and Arnold to Paris to take charge of the school on Mont-Sainte-Geneviève.[49]

Bernard wrote the pope. Not knowing that Arnold was on his way to Paris rather than Rome, he anticipated that both Peter Abelard *and* Arnold of Brescia would soon approach Innocent. The abbot expected his letter to reach the pope before Peter and Arnold did. He warned: "Goliath advances tall of body, girt in the noble accoutrements of war, and preceded by his armour-bearer, Arnold of Brescia."[50] Bernard was confident that Innocent, having exiled Arnold, thoroughly disapproved of him; Peter's association with Arnold might have clinched the pope's decision given that the struggle over civic control between church and commune was crucial. Bernard's letters accomplished their goal.[51]

Bernard, in describing the relationship between Arnold and Peter with a less than appealing simile, wrote: "Scale is joined to scale, and there is no breathing space between."[52] This negative allusion placing the two on the back of Leviathan (Job 41:15-17), nevertheless, reflects strong commitment on the part of Arnold for Abelard and Abelard for Arnold.

Bernard succeeded in obtaining the pope's condemnation of Peter Abelard *and* his writings. The writings concerned Bernard more than Abelard himself. Abelard could be stopped because he was mortal, but books were extremely hard to control and these books were obviously of interest to inquiring minds.

> Although he is no longer lurking in his lair: would that his poisonous writings were still lurking in their shelves, and not being discussed at the crossroads! His books have wings: and they who hate the light because their lives are evil, have dashed into the light thinking it was darkness. Darkness is being brought into towns

---

48. Greenaway, *Arnold*, 76, 77.
49. John of Salisbury, *Historia Pontificalis*, 63. Appendix I.A., 128.
50. Bernard, *Letters*, 239:318. Appendix I.C., 133.
51. Most authorities agree that Bernard drafted the Bishops' Letter as well as his own personal letters to the pope. See for example Poole, *Illustrations*, 164, 165, n. 26. "I make no doubt with Bishop Hefele, that they are all of Bernard's composition, though authorized by the persons to whom they are ascribed."
52. Bernard, *Letters*, 239:318.

and castles in the place of light; and for honey, poison or, I should say, poison in honey is being offered on all sides to everyone. His writings "have passed from country to country, and from one kingdom to another."[53]

Arnold did not go to Rome with Peter, and Peter did not get there. He became ill and was unable travel beyond Cluny. Peter the Venerable, who, the record indicates, deserved the name, saw to the care of Abelard. The news came, Innocent upheld the decision of the bishops and the abbot of Clairvaux, and issued two rescripts (official papal decisions) condemning Peter. The second of them ordered Abelard *and* Arnold to be confined in separate monasteries and their books burned.[54]

Through the efforts of Peter the Venerable, Peter and Bernard were reconciled before Abelard's death.

Teaching Poor Students on Mont-Sainte-Geneviève

Arnold's tempestuous, prophetic, pastoral career was not over. Peter Abelard, who had waged so many battles and had truly been the warrior he envisioned himself to be in his youth, retired from combat and passed his mantle to Arnold, who took his place in Paris. Arnold resumed teaching, continuing the tradition of scholarship, integrity, and self-denial.

He was probably more rigorous than Peter in practicing self-denial and likely placed greater emphasis on social and political concerns. He was less popular than Peter. John of Salisbury reports: "[H]e had no listeners except poor students who publicly begged their bread from door to door to support themselves and their master."[55]

Based on this statement some have concluded that Arnold's teaching career in Paris was not successful. This is unjustified. It is not as if Arnold was looking for wealthy students. Wealth was not something he needed or considered useful. When a student began studying with him, the student was likely encouraged to forsake wealth, if he had any. Arnold did not leave his teaching post in Paris because the school failed.

In the midst of expounding the scriptures at the Church of Saint Hilary, "consistent with the law accepted by Christian people," he made use

---

53. Ibid. Appendix, I.C., 133.
54. Greenaway, 79, 80.
55. John of Salisbury, *Historia Pontificalis*, 64. Appendix I.A., 128.

of his podium to criticize wealthy clergy. "To the bishops he was merciless on account of their avarice and filthy lucre, most of all because of stains on their personal lives, and their striving to build the church of God in blood." In addition to criticizing wealth, Arnold specifically criticized Bernard of Clairvaux. "He denounced the abbot, whose name is renowned above all others for his many virtues, as a seeker after vainglory, envious of all who won distinction in learning or religion unless they were his own disciples."[56]

Arnold's criticism of Bernard was neither gentle nor surprising, given what had occurred at Sens. Conversation about what happened was still in full swing, though without Abelard. Too ill to pursue further combat, Peter had turned his attention to preparing for death.

Peter the Venerable wrote Heloise, "Busy like this the heavenly Visitor found him and summoned him to the wedding feast, his lamps full of oil. He whose unique mastery of learning made his fame known almost all over the world pressed onwards as a meek and humble disciple of Him who said 'learn of Me for I am meek and lowly of heart'. And so he crossed over."[57]

After teaching at Mont-Sainte-Geneviève for a year, Arnold was dislodged by Bernard. "In consequence [of Arnold's denouncements] the abbot prevailed on the most Christian king to expel him from the Frankish kingdom."[58] With Abelard out of the way, Bernard could turn his attention to Arnold, but he had to wait to take action because the verdict of Sens was not popular, and the authorities were unwilling to enforce its stipulations.[59] However, Bishop Stephen of Paris had not liked Abelard, and surely felt no warmer toward Arnold. So, influenced by Stephen and Bernard, King Louis VII exiled Arnold from France.

Again we do not know how Arnold received this message or how he felt about it. We do not know who was still at Mont-Sainte-Geneviève other than Arnold's students and his Augustinian brothers. By now Hyacinth Boboni was back in Rome and the others involved with Abelard had

---

56. Ibid.

57. Peter the Venerable, Epist., IV, 21 as quoted by Murray, *Abelard and St. Bernard*, 46. Murray: "He continued quietly in study and prayer at Cluny until he was afflicted with scabies and was sent to the dependent priory of St. Marcel, near Chalons, to be cured. There he died in 1142. The Abbot Peter wrote to Heloise about him, telling her that in Peter 'servo ac vero Christi philosopho' (the servant and true philosopher of Christ) they had a gift beyond price. 'Germanus himself could not have been more lowly, nor Martin more poor.'"

58. John of Salisbury, *Historia Pontificalis*, 64. Appendix I.A., 128.

59. Greenaway, *Arnold*, 82.

moved along. The manner of John of Salisbury's report of Arnold's activities indicates sympathy and, perhaps, some approval; remember, John was a secretary to Pope Eugenius III, a Cistercian and a supporter of Bernard of Clairvaux.[60] John's commentary shows both commitment to objective reporting and also respect for Arnold. He was also respectful of Bernard, with whom he had a relationship as well.[61] While in the papal court, John had personal contact with Hyacinth and Guido. The four, Arnold, Hyacinth, Guido, and John had been students of Master Peter.[62]

Before leaving Paris, Arnold must have discussed his situation with his students and his brother canons at Mont-Sainte-Geneviève. How did the canon from Brescia come to choose Zurich? Perhaps it was not so much a choice as a call or placement by his order. He was about forty-two years old when he parted with his students and friends and left his teaching ministry in Paris. He must have wondered what Zurich would be like—what the future held for him. With many thoughts, he embarked on another journey—it would not be his last.

Teaching in Zurich

There are three items of evidence regarding Arnold in Zurich: a letter from Bernard of Clairvaux to the bishop of Constance, Otto of Freising's account,[63] and a reference to Arnold's work in Zurich in a letter from Wezel (Wetzel), a spokesman for the Roman Senate, to Frederick Barbarossa, written in 1152.[64] From these sources we know Arnold's teaching in Zurich had significant impact.

60. It was to Eugenius III, the former Bernard of Pisa, to whom Bernard of Clairvaux addressed his treatise on papal rule, *de Consideratione*.

61. Bernard once wrote a letter on John's behalf.

62. John of Salisbury, *Metalogicon*, as quoted by Poole, *Illustrations*, 203: "When as a lad, I first went into Gaul for the cause of study [1136] ... I addressed myself to the Peripatetic of Palais [Abelard], who then presided upon Mount Saint Genovefa, an illustrious teacher and admired of all men. There at his feet I acquired the first rudiments of the dialectical art, and snatched according to the scant measure of my wits, whatever passed his lips with entire greediness of mind."

63. Otto, *Deeds*, 143, 144. "So that man, fleeing from Italy, betook himself to the lands beyond the Alps, and there assuming the role of teacher in Zurich, a town of Swabia, he sowed his pernicious doctrine for some time." How could Otto not have known that Arnold was at Sens? If he did, he forgot to mention it.

64. Wezel's letter is found in Appendix I.F., 140–144, and discussed in Chapter 5. Greenaway discusses it in some detail on page 95ff.

Arnold probably resided at Grossmunster, a house of canons in Zurich.⁶⁵ He continued to teach and preach apostolic poverty and the separation of the church from civil power, as he had in Paris. Perhaps he continued to criticize Bernard. He was well established in Zurich when a letter from Bernard arrived at the residence of the bishop of Constance, Herman of Arbon, who had oversight of Zurich, fifty miles away. Bernard wrote: "It is not to be wondered at that you were not able to foresee the hour or observe the nocturnal entry of the thief."⁶⁶ Making no mention of a Christian community of regular canons with whom Arnold lived, Bernard informed Herman that Arnold was in Zurich by the power of Satan.

The former abbot of San Pietro had been well received, according to the Cistercian abbot. His letter recognized Arnold's popularity and discounted the impressive fruits of his life as merely cover for his so called Satanic mission. "I speak of Arnold of Brescia, a man whom I could wish was as praise-worthy for his doctrine as for his way of life. If you want to know, he is a man who comes neither eating nor drinking, that he may sup alone with the devil on the blood of souls."⁶⁷

Bernard probably learned that Arnold was teaching and preaching in Zurich from Cistercians in the community. In his letter to Bishop Herman, he acknowledged no possibility of integrity or genuine Christian service on Arnold's part. He wrote about Arnold with even greater alarm than he had of the books of Abelard which he had called "foxes." In Zurich, he was convinced, far worse than foxes, a living wolf was loose among the sheep. In the letter, Bernard expressed his primary concern, his fear that Arnold would cause *social and political* upheaval.

The influence of Arnold's prophetic teaching was recalled in a letter we will have reason to consider in another context. In 1152, Wezel, on behalf of the Senate and the Roman Commune, wrote to Frederick Barbarossa, successor of Conrad III to the German throne, and legitimate claimant to the Imperial Crown. In the letter, the purpose of which was to convince the young ruler to seek authorization for his imperial status from the Roman Senate rather than from the pope, Wezel named three well-known people who were supporters of Arnold in Zurich: Rudolf of Ravensburg, Ulrich of Lenzburg, Imperial Prefect at Zurich, and Eberhard of Bodman.⁶⁸

---

65. Greenaway, *Arnold*, 87.
66. Bernard, *Letters*, 250:329–331. Appendix I.C., 134.
67. Ibid.
68. Wezel, letter. Ep. 405:541. In *Epistolae Wibald of Stablo and Corvey*. See also

On the Move

Ulrich was a trusted counselor of Conrad III, who had employed him several times as an envoy.[69] Using his name as a reference in the letter to the young German prince indicates that Ulrich supported Arnold's life and teaching. Ulrich and the others found Arnold's message appealing, supporting as he did the supremacy of the state in secular matters. The combination of scholarship, exemplary living, and his teaching made Arnold attractive to many secular leaders. This is exactly what concerned Bernard and explains why he wrote:

> It is his habit to attract the rich and powerful by soft words and the pretence of virtue, according to those words: "He will agree with the rich to lie in wait at dark corners, and kill the man who never wronged him". When he has obtained their good will and feels sure of their friendship, then you will see the man openly confront the clergy and, with the support of military power, rise up against the bishops themselves, and rage on all sides against the ecclesiastical order.[70]

Although this warning may not have troubled a layman such as Ulrich, it apparently alarmed Bishop Herman, and it reminds us, that although Bernard shared ascetic values with Arnold, he drew the line against anything he thought disruptive of the social order or novel in theology.

After receiving this letter, Bishop Herman ordered Arnold to leave Zurich. The result was slightly less than Bernard hoped, however. His letter continued:

> Knowing this, I do not see what better or more wholesome thing you can do than to follow the advice of the Apostle and 'put away the evil one from amongst you', though the friend of the Bridegroom will *see that he is imprisoned rather than put to flight* [emphasis added], so that he should not be able to run around doing any more harm . . . If we are warned by the scriptures to catch the little foxes which spoil the vine, how much more is a great and fierce wolf to be bound fast so that he shall not break into the fold and slay and destroy the sheep.[71]

In spite of Bernard's passion, Arnold was not imprisoned as Bernard wanted. But he was forced to move on.

Appendix I.F. and Greenaway, *Arnold*, 95.

69. Greenaway, Ibid.
70. Bernard, *Letters*, 250:329–331.
71. Ibid.

Respite in Passau

We would know nothing of Arnold's life between the time he left Zurich in 1143 and his arrival in Rome in 1146 were it not for another letter from Bernard. He had once again hunted down the "wolf" and was determined to protect the church from the "beast."

We learn that Arnold had been received and may for a time have been hosted by Cardinal Guido (Guy), who was on a legatine mission in Passau, a town in Bohemia. Legates had the authority of the pope wherever they were sent. The fact that Guido received and housed Arnold indicates there were others in the curia who remained sympathetic to the teaching of Abelard and who respected Arnold as a colleague of Abelard. Arnold had gained a reputation in the eyes of some influential churchmen as a worthy scholar and servant of Jesus. Guido, Hyacinth, and Guy of Castello, who had supported Peter Abelard, knew Arnold personally. Guy, as we know, was in Paris in 1139 and 1140, just prior to Sens, and he succeeded Innocent II as Pope Celestine II in 1143.[72]

The monastery of St. Nicholas was a well-established house of canons in Passau founded by St. Altmann, who was Bishop of Passau from 1065 to 1091.[73] St. Nicholas was renowned for its care of souls, so much so that it was difficult for its canons to pursue the contemplative life. "Because of the very frequent interruptions through hearing confessions, visiting the sick and certain other employments, we are not able to observe silence according to the customs of other canons."[74] This may have been Arnold's residence while he was in Passau.

Bernard's letter to Guido was much like the one to the bishop of Constance. He wrote that Arnold is "the man whose life is as sweet as honey and whose doctrine is as bitter as poison, the man with the head of a dove and the tail of a scorpion, the man whom Brescia has ejected, Rome rejected, and France repulsed; whom Germany abhors, and Italy will not receive."[75]

Bernard could imagine only two reasons for Guido to extend hospitality to Arnold: "either I must believe that he is not at all known to you, or (what is more likely) that you have hopes of converting him. But who can fashion a son of Abraham from this stone?" Apparently, Bernard's sources have informed him that Arnold and Guido are close or, at the very least, Guido has

---

72. Luscombe, *School*, 21.
73. Dickinson, *The Origin of the Austin Canons*, 45.
74. Ibid., 58. Dickinson makes reference to this quotation on page 184 as well.
75. Bernard, *Letters*, 251:331, 332. Appendix, I.C., 136.

been hospitable to the canon, because Bernard wrote: "to be friendly with him, to hold him often in conversation, not to say to entertain him, looks like favoring him, and is a powerful protection for any enemy. A friend of the Apostolic legate and member of his household will put forward with impunity what he likes, and will be readily believed whatever he says."[76]

The abbot reminded Guido of Arnold's history and asked, "Who is there amongst those with whom he is driven to take refuge who does not heartily wish him back again in his own country?" and "what possible excuse can there be for flouting the judgment of the Supreme Pontiff? . . . And so, to favour this man is to contradict the Pope and even the Lord God." He concluded: "I have every confidence in your prudence and uprightness and do not doubt that, when you have learned the truth of the matter from this letter, you will be firm and act in a way that is becoming to yourself and beneficial to the Church of God, on whose behalf you are discharging the office of legate. You command my affection and may count upon my service."[77]

Bernard was aware that he was writing to someone who might judge the matter quite differently—indeed, a prominent clergyman who possibly shared Arnold's and Abelard's criticisms of himself, rather than his opinion of them. Signs indicate that this letter, unlike its predecessor, failed to accomplish its author's purpose. Arnold was not asked to leave Passau, and may have remained there until either 1145 or 1146, when he traveled to Viterbo to meet with Eugenius III. Or, he may have returned to Italy sometime in 1143, shortly after the death of Innocent, as John of Salisbury's comment suggests.

With Celestine, the former Guy of Castello and, as pope, collector of Peter Abelard's writings, the atmosphere must have been quite different for Arnold. We have no evidence to help us determine how long he stayed in Passau or where he lived if he left Passau prior to his trip to Viterbo. It is unlikely he was involved in anything controversial during these years—nothing is mentioned and Pope Eugenius was willing to reconcile Arnold to the church in 1145 or 1146.

Wherever Arnold spent the years 1143 to 1146, we can be confident that he was engaged as a canon, teaching, preaching, and studying. His relationship with Guido seems to have prepared him for reconciliation. Guido represented honest inquiry and sound churchmanship. Arnold went forward from that experience, we believe, hoping for a renewed relationship with the church now that it had a pope who, he hoped, would seek essential change.

76. Ibid.
77. Ibid.

5

Pastor of the Republic of Rome

THE ELECTION OF POPE Eugenius III (late 1080s–1153), formerly Bernard of Pisa, on February 15, 1145, surprised Latin Christendom. He was a relatively unknown monk, the abbot of the Cistercian house of St. Anastasius that was located on the road from Rome to Porto.

Bernard of Clairvaux feared that the new pope, though a friend to whom he had been mentor, was too innocent to handle the difficult and complex problems of the papacy. He wrote to the Roman Curia after hearing the news of Eugenius's election:

> God have mercy on you; what have you done? . . . Why have you thwarted the hopes of a needy man, why have you confused the decisions of a poor man, a beggar, a penitent? . . . What reason, what counsel, made you, as soon as the late Pope had died, suddenly rush upon this rustic, lay hands upon him when in hiding from the world, and knocking away his axe, mattock or hoe, drag him to the palatine, place him upon a throne, clothe him in purple and fine linen, and gird him with a sword "ready to take vengeance upon the heathen, to curb nations, to chain kings, and bind princes in fetters?" Had you no other wise and experienced man amongst you who would have been better suited to these things?[1]

Bernard could write! One wonders how Eugenius felt when he read this letter, as he surely must have. Also, note the items Bernard quoted as papal tasks. It described closely what Arnold regretfully saw the popes doing.

---

1. Bernard, *Letters*, 315:385.

Bernard waited in vain to hear from Eugenius after his election, and, not hearing, wrote him:

> The whole church rejoices and glorifies God, because she has a confidence in you such as she does not seem to have had for a long time in your predecessors. But especially does she rejoice who bore you in her womb and suckled you at her breast. And why should not I too rejoice? Why should not I be one of those who are glad?
>
> I do indeed rejoice but I confess that I do so not without trembling. I rejoice indeed, but in the very act of rejoicing fear and trembling come upon me. Although I have laid aside the name of father [he had been Eugenius's spiritual father], neither the fears not the anxieties of a father have left me, least of all the affection and heart of a father. When I think of the heights to which you have been lifted up, I fear the danger which is at hand. I do not think that the words "Man when he is honoured does not remember what he is" refer so much to the time as to the cause and mean that honours blind the judgement of a man, so that he forgets that he is human.[2]

Bernard went on to express hope that the new pope would be like the original shepherd "who could say with a clear conscience and a pure heart: 'Silver and gold have I none.'"[3] On the matter of personal wealth, Bernard and Arnold were in agreement.

The humble monk, however, stepped into his new role—one might say new persona—as Pope Eugenius III with surprising vigor and authority. He faced a very difficult situation. For example, his predecessor, Lucius II, had led papal troops in an attack upon the Roman Capitol in hopes of reestablishing papal authority. Reportedly hit by a stone, Lucius died a few days later.[4]

Problems facing Eugenius included: the rebellious Roman commune, difficult relations with the Norman king of Sicily to the south, rebellious nobles of the papal states, and issues relating to the German kings beginning with Conrad III and the Holy Roman Empire. One wonders, with such an agenda, how the the pope found time to attend to spiritual matters.

In addition to these pressing concerns, the pope had to deal with daily administration of the church and its growing desire to recover lost lands in the East, eventually leading to the Second Crusade. It is hard to imagine a

---

2. Ibid., 205:278.
3. Ibid., 279.
4. Gregorovius, *Rome in the Middle Ages*, Vol. IV—Part II, 491.

tougher job and it isn't difficult to understand why Bernard of Clairvaux worried about his little brother-in-Christ taking it on.

Arnold of Brescia's life was also greatly affected by the movements and forces of the time. And, like Pope Eugenius, he was soon in the middle of things, occupying a role of far greater significance than he had imagined.

Probably under the influence of Cardinal Guido in Passau, Arnold came to an understanding that led him to seek reconciliation with the papacy and the church. We speculate how this came about, mindful that evidence at hand cannot confirm our historical imaginations.[5]

First, consider that Innocent II, Arnold's enemy of long standing, had died. Their relationship had been unsatisfactory in the extreme. Innocent had stifled the commune movement in Brescia, exiled Arnold from Italy, and, in striking down Abelard's appeal without a personal hearing, issued an order disciplining Arnold as well. It is not hard to understand why Arnold did not envision reconciliation as long as Innocent was head of the church, and how unlikely for Innocent to have granted reconciliation to Arnold if requested.

Over time, the hospitality of Guido and election of Guy of Castello as Pope Celestine II (unknown–1144) changed Arnold. It became possible for him to converse civilly with persons who held positions of authority, including the position of greatest ecclesiastical authority—pope. There is no record of conversations between Arnold and Pope Celestine or others in the curia, but with old friends there, conversations might well have occurred. As for correspondence, everything Arnold wrote was burned, leaving no clues on that front, at least from his side.

Celestine's administration only lasted a few months, not long enough for anything to happen, and Arnold did not seek reconciliation with Celestine's successor, Lucius II, suggesting that he let such matters go in favor of continuing his duties as a canon in Passau or perhaps somewhere in Italy, possibly even Brescia.[6] He did not seek papal blessing until after the election of Eugenius.

Eugenius III was a spiritual man uninterested in worldly vices, wealth, or power. There were many who thought he represented a new age for the church and the papacy—a fresh start. Later developments led to a rift

---

5. On the role of imatination in exploring history, see: Collingwood, *The Idea of History*, 231–249.

6. John of Salisbury reported, as noted above, that Arnold returned to Italy after the death of Innocent.

between Arnold and Eugenius, but at the time of their reconciliation in 1146[7] they apparently supported one another.

And so it was that these two men, one a faithful Cistercian, and the other a faithful Austin canon, met at Viterbo, a safe, friendly environment for the pope behind the city walls, to reconcile in Christian brotherhood. Would that we could listen in on their conversation. Eugenius and the Senate had negotiated a concordat in 1145 that recognized the Roman Republic and the Senate.[8] In turn the Senate allowed restoration of the office of prefect, a city manager with considerable power, appointed by the pope.[9] Arnold probably thought Eugenius's recognition of the Republic was a step in the right direction.

The pope sent Arnold to Rome to perform penance by fasting and vigils and prayers in the holy places in the City. He did the prescribed penance, took a solemn oath to show obedience,[10] and reentered the fold of Mother Church, only to fall out again within a year or so. What happened?

In his chronicle, Otto of Freising reports: "But when [Arnold] learned of the death of Innocent he entered the City, near the beginning of the pontificate of Eugenius. . . . He incessantly and irreverently perpetrated these things and others like them for many days (that is, from the death of Celestine until this time)."[11]

Otto's version is misleading and he contradicts himself. He has Arnold coming to Rome in 1144 which, though possible, is not corroborated, and, more to the point, he gives Arnold a role in stirring up the city against Eugenius *prior* to their reconciliation. However, historians who have had the benefit of *Historia Pontificalis* (Poole, Gregorovius, Giesebrecht, Abbe Vacandard, Ugo Balzani, Greenaway, Frugoni, and Alfieri to mention a

---

7. It cannot be determined for certain whether Arnold and Eugenius reconciled in 1145 or 1146. Poole gives several solid reasons for 1146. 1) The pope was in Viterbo from May 23 to the end of 1146. 2) Bernard of Clairvaux is silent about Arnold in relation to the tumults of Rome prior to 1146. 3) John of Salisbury is "so extraordinarily precise that one is led to believe that he heard the particulars very soon after Arnold was received back, and John can hardly have been employed in the Papal service until the autumn of 1146." Poole, H.P. Introduction, lxiv, lxv.

8. Alfieri, *Story of Brescia*, 596. Alfieri thinks that Eugenius "pardoned Arnold and let him enter Rome, hoping perhaps to find in him a repentant and perfectly qualified mediator for settling the controversy with the commune."

9. Greenaway, *Arnold*, 117.

10. John of Salisbury, *Historia Pontificalis*, 64.

11. Otto of Freising, *Deeds*, 144. Appendix I.B., 131.

few) are agreed that Arnold was not politically involved with the Senate prior to 1147.

A careful reading of John of Salisbury's account suggests more than one meeting between Arnold and Eugenius. John reported that Arnold

> returned to Italy after Innocent's death and, after promising reparation and obedience to the Roman church, was received at Viterbo by Pope Eugenius. Penance was imposed on him, which he claimed to have performed [performed before his meeting with the pope?] in fasts, vigils and prayers in the holy places of the city; and *again* [emphasis added] he took a solemn oath to show obedience.[12]

According to this, Arnold requested reconciliation prior to meeting the pope at Viterbo. If so, maybe an initial request was made in writing; possibly Guido or a colleague approached the pope on Arnold's behalf; maybe a message was carried to Eugenius by Arnold's Augustinian brothers.

In any event, Arnold went to Rome, did penance, returned to the pope, promised obedience, and reconciliation was confirmed. John moved on quickly to report: "Whilst dwelling in Rome under pretext of penance he won the city to his side, and preaching all the more freely because the lord pope was occupied in Gaul he built up a faction known as the heretical sect of the Lombards."[13]

Reflection and research suggest that John condensed the story. He said Arnold began to preach freely while Eugenius was occupied in Gaul. Eugenius left Viterbo for Pisa early in 1147 and departed from there through Lombardy to France in March.[14] As noted, scholars agree that Arnold did not actively oppose the pope until 1147 and, as we shall see, the pope did not take any formal action against him until the summer of 1148. How did Arnold's opposition to the pope come about?

Back to John of Salisbury who fills us in on Arnold's activities leading to the breakup:

12. John of Salisbury, *Historia Pontificalis*, 64. Appendix, I.A., 128.
13. Ibid.
14. Gregorovius, *Rome in the Middle Ages*, 500. Both Gregorovius and Poole qualify the conclusion of some writers that Eugenius fled to France. Gregorovius: "Eugenius had fled but had not been driven away by force of arms"(501). Poole: "His departure has been spoken of as a flight, and it is true that in the spring of 1146 he had fled from Rome. But at Viterbo he had no cause for uneasiness, and it is likely that his primary motive for visiting France was that he might preside over preparations for the Second Crusade." H.P. Preface, xii.

> He had disciples who imitated his austerities and won favour with the populace through outward decency and austerity of life, but found their chief supporters amongst pious women. He himself was frequently heard on the Capitol and in public gatherings. He had already publicly denounced the cardinals, saying that their college, by its pride, avarice, hypocrisy and manifold shame was not the church of God, but a place of business and den of thieves, which took the place of the scribes and Pharisees amongst Christian peoples.[15]

Apparently Arnold did not mince words.

Before proceeding farther along Arnold's trail, let's attend to questions that may help us understand his transition from church outsider to insider and back to outsider to prepare us for what is ahead. First: How was Arnold able to come to an understanding that allowed him in good conscience to become reconciled to the papacy? Second: How did he justify breaking the ensuing oath of obedience?

With regard to the first question, Arnold's experience with Guido in Passau gave him a vision of what could be possible in the church. Guido became a friend who ignored attempts to dislodge or disown Arnold, even with pressure from so powerful a quarter as Bernard of Clairvaux. He was someone who, it seems, Arnold knew to be as authentic as he himself intended to be. Guido was at the heart of the church—a papal legate, a representative of the pope. Hospitality given and received nourished everything. These men must have had many conversations about the church. Guido, even though some distance from the Vatican, was in the information pipe line. In his presence, Arnold was not a renegade—exactly what Bernard feared.

Furthermore, Bernard of Pisa, the new pope, was known to be humble, poor, a person fulfilling his vows, and doing the work of God. He did not seem like someone who would throw his weight around. Arnold was familiar with the new pope's convictions and background. With Eugenius's leadership Arnold must have felt hope for a purified church dedicated to service and the care of souls, freed from the hindrances of wealth and secular power. This is a plausible answer to the first question.

Let's move on to the second question. How and why, after reconciliation, did Arnold break his oath of obedience? While the conflict between the pope and the City of Rome renewed, Eugenius increasingly accepted the inevitable political responsibilities of the papacy. He dedicated himself to matters like organizing a crusade while ministry and reform slipped off

---

15. John of Salisbury, *Historia Ponticalis,* 64, 65. See also Appendix I.A., 128, 129.

center stage, and to manipulating, as best he could, King Roger of Sicily, his main ally. Surely Arnold wondered why a spiritual leader needed such allies. And, as he witnessed the continued opulence of the clergy, it must have become increasingly difficult for him to think of these men, including the pope, as Christ's servants trying to live like Jesus. Clearly, it was a system still going astray.

There is a story about what might have been the final break between Arnold and Eugenius told by the writer Walter Map (ca. 1140–1208 or 1210), a clergyman and courtier of King Henry II of England. Two Cistercian abbots and Map were among the guests at a dinner hosted by Thomas Moore, Archbishop of Canterbury, sometime between 1162 and 1164. After dinner, one of the Cistercians read, as praiseworthy, a defamatory letter Bernard of Clairvaux had written about Arnold of Brescia. In response, some dinner guests who did not like Bernard took the podium to tell unflattering stories about him.

Map defended Arnold—whether at the dinner as well as in his written account, we can't be sure. He praised Arnold's preaching and teaching and related what happened at a banquet Arnold had attended with cardinals and the pope. This would have been *after* reconciliation.

"[Arnold] finally came to the papal court and saw the tables of the cardinals loaded with vessels of silver and gold, and the dainties at their feasts; in the presence of their lord the Pope he chided them kindly, but they bore it unkindly and cast him out; he returned to the city and began to teach without flagging."[16]

If true, this may have been the breaking point between the pope and Arnold. By ejecting Arnold was it Eugenius, rather than Arnold, who ended their reconciliation? Who broke the covenant? Did such an action free Arnold from his oath of obedience? According to the story, it was the gathered assembly, including the pope, who became angry and violent.[17] They *cast out* Arnold, and he returned to Rome.

---

16. Map, *Courtiers Trifles*, 49, 50. The full text of Map's comments about Arnold can be found in Appendix I.E., 139, 140.

17. This raises the question of time and place. Initially, the story seems to be set in Rome but the phrase "he returned to the city" means it was elsewhere. The story is not as precise as we would like, but it clearly refers to a *definite* occasion when Arnold spoke to the cardinals in the presence of the pope, at a particular dinner. If the dinner took place in Viterbo, for example, it occurred after May of 1146. It could not have been before the reconciliation.

The Roman people heard that Arnold had rebuked the pope and members of the clergy to their faces and had been cast out. The people applauded him. The commune respected Arnold and began to engage him in their cause. Some Romans protested openly on Arnold's behalf. Not willing to take this, Eugenius condemned Arnold. Nothing new for Arnold. It meant, like it or not, the agreement between himself and the pope was null and void.

Let's linger to imagine Arnold at the scene when he "chided" the clergy. What did he do? Did he get up during dinner, tap a goblet or clear his throat, and begin to speak? Was there a ruckus? Did the clergy toss food at him? What did "cast out" mean? Map portrayed Arnold as bold and honorable in contrast to the portrayal of him in Bernard's letter of invective.[18]

Assuming this story circulated at the time, it must have embarrassed Eugenius. For him, the humble monk from Pisa, who neither needed nor asked for anything, to be thought of as the center of opulence must have caused him pain, anger, and consternation. We are told that Eugenius continued to wear his Cistercian habit under his vestments for his entire papacy,[19] indicating his intention to be humble and poor before Christ.

Arnold and Eugenius no longer saw eye-to-eye. Arnold must have decided he could wait no longer for the pope to implement genuine reform. Arnold was a preacher—it was part of his ministry as a canon regular—so he proceeded to preach, and the Roman people wanted to hear what he had to say.

The pope departed Viterbo for France to raise money and preach a crusade. The Arnold-friendly Senate governed the city of Rome, and Arnold preached publicly.

The City Republic

Rome, although no longer the seat of the empire, was famous, perhaps the most famous city in the world. The twelfth-century Renaissance brought Rome, ancient and current, to people's minds again in a fresh way. Pilgrims regularly made their way to see the sights and worship at the churches and shrines.[20]

---

18. Map, *Courtiers' Trifles*, 49, 50.
19. Gregorovius, *Rome in the Middle Ages*, 523.
20. *Mirabilia Urbis Roma* was the chief guidebook to Rome of this time and there were others. Rome was still a sight to see. See Gregorovius, 463–477 and Haskins,

The City itself was in a peculiar position. The cities of Lombardy had healthier economies. In Lombard cities, a burgher class of merchants and artisans had emerged earlier, created communes, and provided new civic leadership. Rome, by contrast, had little industry or commerce. The burgher class was small and slow to form. In addition, the City, by an assumed divine right and the forged Donation of Constantine, was governed by the pope. Other cities had their bishops but Rome's bishop was bishop of the world. The Prefecture, appointed and invested by the pope and, some have suggested, by the emperor as well, administered the City. This was the situation prior to the uprising of the commune.

Gregorovius comments, "The sight of free republics [the Italian communes] irritated the Romans. At a time when so many other cities had renounced episcopal authority, their city remained under the sovereignty of a bishop."[21] During the preceding decades a burgher class had begun to take shape in Rome, and in the 1140s, the lesser nobles, jealous of the aristocratic, ruling nobles, joined the burghers. Together they became the new commune that seized the Capitol in 1143 and declared the revival of the Senate.[22] Thus the populace—the burghers, the lower ranks of the clergy, and the lower ranks of the nobility—joined together against the pope, the higher ranks of the clergy, and the aristocracy.[23]

A struggle with the city of Tivoli, a smaller city east of Rome, triggered the Roman revolution. The Tivolese desired their independence, while Rome regarded the city as its vassal. In 1141, Roman troops were defeated trying to discipline Tivoli, which deeply embarrassed and angered the Romans. In 1143, in concert with the pope and his troops, the Romans did defeat Tivoli and planned to apply heavy sanctions. From the Roman point of view, the pope was overly inclined to clemency; he would not allow the walls of Tivoli to be torn down. Roman anger at the pope was the spark that ignited the revolution. The burghers and the lower ranks of the nobility took control of the city, established themselves in the Capitol, revived the Roman Senate, and deposed the pope's Prefecture.

The sources agree that the new senators were short on knowledge; nevertheless, the Romans took the revival of the Senate seriously. They knew little history and had a limited understanding of the actual political and social

---

Renaissance, 117–124.

21. Gregorovius, *Rome in the Middle Ages*, 454.
22. Ibid., 462.
23. Ibid., 505, 506.

forces at work in their own time. They did, however, know, claim, and believe in the tradition of the Roman Senate and the Roman Empire. According to Robert Benson, they audaciously claimed to be not only the duly established government of Rome, as in the other cities governed by communes, but also the center of authority in the Holy Roman Empire.[24]

During 1144, Jordan Pierleone, the nephew of the antipope Anacletus II, became instrumental in developing and articulating the philosophy and program of the commune. He was the only member of a noble family to join the commune at that time, and likely the most educated and most influential person in its ranks.

The pope, the pope's ally the king of Sicily, and the Roman nobles constantly opposed the Senate. As Benson observes, "[T]he revolutionaries urgently needed an ally."[25] They looked to the kings of Germany—the rulers who were candidates for the crown of Holy Roman Emperor. Beginning in 1144 the Senate sent a number of letters to King Conrad III (1093–1152), appealing to him for support. These letters have been lost.[26]

Keep in mind that this all happened *before* Arnold arrived in Rome. When he joined the cause of the Senate and commune in 1147, he brought to the Senate classical knowledge along with convictions that greatly strengthened and clarified their philosophy and stimulated the movement.

The Senate urged King Conrad to ally himself with Rome rather than Pope Eugenius, because, they warned the king, the pope's alliances and flirtations with the Norman king of Sicily were a major threat to him. The Senate contended that the emperor's logical ally was the City of Rome, not the pope, and that Rome could be of great service to the emperor.

When Eugenius was elected pope in 1145, the Senate would not allow him to he be consecrated in Rome without recognizing the independence of the City, which he was not willing to do. He took refuge in the monastery of Farfa, where he was consecrated on the fourth of March. From there he went to Viterbo to reside.[27]

The Romans were unable to extend their sovereignty over other cities. An alliance of the neighboring cities, Tivoli in particular,[28] and the aris-

---

24. Benson, "Political *Renovatio*: Two Models," 341. "As a case history the Commune [of Rome] holds particular interest, for it furnishes the twelfth century's only example of political classicism at the very center of a historical movement."

25. Ibid.

26. Ibid.

27. Ugo Balzani, *The Popes and the Hohenstaufen*, 13, 14.

28. Gregorovius, *Rome in the Middle Ages*, 495.

tocrats of Rome, who feared for their countryside possessions, forced the City to receive the pope back. In addition, they forced Rome to abolish the Patrician office held by Jordan Pierlione, restore the Prefect, and recognize the sovereignty of the pope.[29]

Shortly before Christmas, Eugenius left Sutri, a city located between Rome and Viterbo, and journeyed to Rome. He entered triumphantly and celebrated Christmas at the Lateran.

Although this may have seemed like the end of the rebellion, and the end of the commune as well, it was not. The pope and the Senate signed the treaty allowing the Senate to continue governing the City, which, in turn, acknowledged it was under the pope's investiture. The treaty was advantageous to both parties. "The city commune," observes Gregorovius, "had thus wrung its recognition from the Pope, and the Pope on his part had preserved the principle of his government, since from him the Senate received investiture."[30]

The Senate, comprised of fifty-six (the number varied) senators elected mainly from the burgher class (even though many nobles had by now joined the commune), took the right of coinage from the pope, and for the first time since ancient days, silver coins were minted bearing the inscription *Senatus populusque Romanus*"—"the Roman Senate and People." It must have been exciting for the people of the City to have these coins.

"The full Senate formed the great council or *Consistorium,* and a committee of *Consiliatores* or *Procuratores* of the republic was placed at its head."[31] According to Gregorovius the Senate possessed legislative power and the committee of *Consiliatores* exercised executive power. The Senate also administered civil justice. Under this treaty, the Senate and commune were now legitimate.

Eugenius's stay in the city was brief, however. The Romans clamored to extend their authority, and the higher nobles and higher clergy were angry about the role of the Senate. Tivoli created more problems, and the Romans called for it to be destroyed. The pope allowed Tivoli's walls to be pulled down this time, but that did not satisfy the Romans. At the end of January, 1146, the pope fled to St. Angelo; then he moved on to Sutri in March. In May, he proceeded to Viterbo.

---

29. Balzani, *The Popes and the Hohenstaufen,* 15.
30. Gregorovius, *Rome in the Middle Ages,* 496.
31. Ibid., 497.

Arnold arrived soon after Eugenius took residence in Viterbo. The two men reconciled at this time, according to Poole and others, and, as a condition of reconciliation, Eugenius sent Arnold to Rome to do penance and take up residence.

Arnold in the Republic of Rome, Phase I

Which house of regular canons did Arnold enter in Rome? There were at least two choices: St. John Lateran and St. Croce in Gerusalemme, in Urbe.[32] For the first time since he was exiled from Brescia—seven years earlier—he was completely *regular*—that is, legitimate.

The arrangements under the treaty of 1145 between the pope and Rome must have seemed relatively satisfactory to Arnold. Although the pope had retained investiture, he was not exercising governing power in Rome. The appropriate people, the senators, were in charge of secular matters.

If we follow Walter Map's story, we conclude that it was the lifestyle of the curia and higher clergy, rather than politics, that Arnold first reacted against. During 1146, it seems quite safe to conclude, Arnold preached and taught as a canon regular while praying at the holy sites. As time passed he became a more public figure. He had classical knowledge; he had read the Latin classics, very likely Cicero, Ovid, Livy, Tacitus, Horace, Seneca, and others. One can easily see why he became an important resource to the Senate.

Eugenius left Viterbo in 1147, and made his way through Italy to France promoting a Second Crusade. This drew Eugenius and Bernard of Clairvaux together in common cause in the type of activity that was Bernard's forte. He had traveled and preached throughout Europe on behalf of Innocent II against the antipope Anacletus, and now he traveled and preached to raise an army.

It was Bernard who convinced a reluctant King Conrad to join the Crusade. "[A] more than usually eloquent sermon of St. Bernard's seemed to overcome [Conrad's] hesitation, so that, much moved and in tears, he interrupted the Saint in order to offer himself to God and take up the cross." In this matter, observed Balzani, Bernard's zeal exceeded the wishes of the pope, who would have preferred Conrad to remain in Europe to look after Germany, restore papal authority in Rome, and receive the imperial crown.[33]

---

32. Dickinson, *The Origin of the Austin Canons*, 41.
33. Balzani, *The Popes and the Hohenstaufen*, 18, 19.

Arnold, of course, opposed the Crusade. To him it was double dipping in secular affairs—not only did the church exercise secular governance, which it should not, but it also promoted war! It appears that the people and parties of Rome had little interest in the Crusade; the attention the Crusade required from the pope and the king afforded the Senate an opportunity to attend to its affairs with little interference; the needs of church and people were of greater importance to Arnold than military affairs and world politics.

As time passed, Arnold's involvement with the Senate deepened. The power in Arnold's preaching and his way of life attracted people who were serious about religion. While the pope was occupied in Gaul raising money and preaching the Crusade, Arnold preached freely. His followers, known as the heretical sect of the Lombards, imitated his austerities and won favor with the populace through *decency* [emphasis added] and austerity of life. Many of his chief supporters were women.[34] High praise, given Arnold's values.

Ignoring the implied diminishment of John's words, Arnold's preaching led to a dedicated lay movement involving both men and women. Participation in the "sect" of the Lombards (sometimes referred to as Arnoldists) was not restricted to the laity. "Lower" clergy, canons of the Augustinian houses, and parish priests were certainly involved as well. Arnold was hard on hierarchy.

Women took leadership and provided major support; ordinary people responded to Arnold; apparently he could move freely and personally among the citizens, cross barriers between classes and levels of education, and converse easily with people. He was in touch with the common things of life and had good, loyal friends among the poor, to whom he was loyal as well.

These conclusions rest upon his acknowledged power as a preacher, and the fact that among those who openly identified with him were poor students in Paris and lay persons—both women and men—in Rome. His following was diverse and wide spread; it included many with little social prestige or financial resources.

In his letter "To the Roman People," Bernard of Clairvaux alleged that the Romans looted the churches when they forced Eugenius out of the city in 1146.[35] He deplored both the looting and their hostility to their bishop.

---

34. John of Salisbury, *Historia Pontificalis*, 64. Appendix I.A., 128.

35. See Bernard's letter, "To the Roman People, When they Rebelled Against Pope Eugenius," James, letter 319:391–394 or Mabillon, Vol. 2, letter CCXLLIII:712–717. In

Pastor of the Republic of Rome

If looting occurred, Arnold was surely as much against it as Bernard. Arnold had little use for money, thought it a hindrance to spiritual life, and considered wealth anathema to religious orders. We can safely reject any suggestion that Arnold had a role in, or encouraged, looting and violence. In fact, the letter may have been written before Arnold came to Rome.

About the same time Bernard wrote to the people of the City (1146), he also wrote to King Conrad urging him to extend his might to force the Romans into line under their bishop:

> The pride and arrogance of the Romans exceeds their strength. And, I ask you, would any great and powerful person, be he a king or an emperor, presume to conduct himself so abominably against both the empire and the Church? But this accursed and lawless people, who know not their own limitations, and do not stop to think or ponder on the purpose or result of their actions, in their folly and frenzy have dared to attempt this enormous sacrilege. God forbid that this mob rule, this audacity of the common people, should prevail for one moment against the king.[36]

Conrad was neither in a position nor a frame of mind to respond to Bernard's plea. He probably shared Bernard's estimate of the Roman people, but may not have been especially unhappy about the pope's difficulties. Whatever the reasons, the commune was untroubled by either pope or king until 1149. During that time Arnold's influence and care for the people flourished.

What was the content of Arnold's sermons during these years? We know he preached against the wealth and political aspirations of the clergy, but what was he preaching and teaching to comfort people? To call them to discipleship? To care for one another? Did he preach love of God and neighbor? Did he pursue conversation? What did he do to foster education?

Abbot Bernard urged people to conversion, meaning conversion to monastic life, particularly to the Cistercian Order.[37] Arnold, also, called for

---

Mabillon's edition, the letter is introduced by this paragraph: "At the instigation of Arnald of Brescia, the Romans tried to establish the ancient Republican liberty in the place of the Pope's authority, leaving him only tithes and free-will offerings." Once again Arnold is erroneously accused of initiating the Roman revolution before he was in fact involved. Bernard does not mention Arnold in this letter, an opportunity he was unlikely to miss if he knew Arnold was involved. Mabillon dates this letter 1146. It would not have been later, but one wonders if the looting of the churches, if there was looting, might have occurred earlier, perhaps in 1145.

36. Bernard, "To Conrad, King of the Romans," James, 394, 395, and Mabillon, 717–719.

37. Bernard of Clairvaux, *Sermons on Conversion*. See the introduction, 12,

the clergy to convert to apostolic poverty and, most likely, to common life. However, the life he called for was not restricted to clergy or religious. Lay women and men, the sect of the Lombards, and Arnoldists are not names for religious orders. They are terms that refer primarily to lay people; the impulse of his vision of genuine reform was democratic. People loved it. Arnold's spiritual philosophy was different; it promoted liberty.

The Roman commune and Arnold's activities became openly oppositional to the pope in 1147. The early years of Arnold's ministry in Rome, even after 1147, were devoted primarily to issues of the church and Christian living. He supported the Senate and provided historical, philosophical, and theological foundation for its position and role. The Senate appreciated this assistance and the pastoral care provided by Arnold and the canons regular throughout the city. Thus Arnold and the Senate entered into a pact of mutual support sometime prior to 1149, but probably after the summer of 1148, when Eugenius went a step further and actually excommunicated Arnold.

John of Salisbury wrote about Arnold in the context of negotiations between the pope and the Romans in 1149. "[Arnold] was said to have bound himself by oath to uphold the honour of the city and Roman republic. The Romans in their turn promised him aid and counsel against all men, and explicitly against the lord pope; for the Roman church had excommunicated him and ordered him to be shunned as a heretic."[38]

As to the Crusade, Eugenius and Bernard recruited an army that proceeded to the Holy Land in late 1147. However, the army was unsuccessful. Conrad, seriously wounded, was lucky to escape with his life; by late 1148, the Crusaders had returned, defeated. This defeat was a severe setback to the pope and to Bernard. Book II of *On Consideration* by Bernard begins with "An Apologia on the Plight of Jerusalem."

> [F]or we have entered a difficult period, as you well know, which appears to herald an end almost to our very existence, not to mention our endeavors. Clearly, the Lord, provoked by our sins, seems in some way to have judged the earth before the appointed time, justly, of course, but unmindful of his mercy. He neither spared his people nor his own name. Are they not saying among the nations, "Where is their God?" And no wonder, for the sons of the Church, and those who are called by the Christian name, lie prostrate in the desert, slain by the sword or destroyed by hunger.[39]

"'Conversion' must be taken in its traditional sense of 'becoming a monk.'"
   38. John of Salisbury, *Historia Pontificalis*, 63. Appendix I.A., 127.
   39. Bernard of Clairvaux, *On Consideration*, 47.

If defeat came from something that displeased the Almighty, Arnold knew what it was—the system. It was the church wielding secular power and promoting wars.

Pope Eugenius, like Bernard, must have been shaken by this defeat. Things were not going well for him. He remained at odds with the commune and made no attempt to return to Rome. He was able to raise money in France and held a council in Reims. After the council, he returned to Italy and resided, ironically, in Brescia from July 15 to September of 1148.

It was from Brescia that Eugenius issued the rescript excommunicating the huge obstacle to his making peace with Rome—the so-called heretic Arnold. He officially removed all doubt regarding Arnold's standing with the church. The commune was ordered, likely not for the first time, to expel him. The papal edict stipulated severe penalties to anyone, specifically including clergy, who had dealings with Arnold. Any clergy who did would lose his benefice and be deprived of priestly office.[40] Eugenius intended to deter the apparently significant support among the cadre of clergy in Rome serving the City alongside Arnold.

Pastor of the Republic, Phase II

The Pact Between the Senate and Arnold

The pope's action altered Arnold's situation. Again one wonders how he felt and what he thought. He must have felt sad, but he might have been amused as well. This was nothing new for him. The church was going down the wrong path and taking the people along with it—curtailing their freedom. The pope's formal action may have deepened Arnold's commitment to kindness and compassion, to comfort the needy, and free people to pursue enterprise.

He was more secure than in the past; ecclesiastical action, even by the pope, could not dislodge him. The Senate refused to obey the rescript of excommunication; instead, it affirmed Arnold's ministry by entering into a pact with him that must have included Rome's clergy. Arnold "bound himself by oath to uphold the honour of the city and Roman republic. The Romans in their turn promised him aid and counsel against all men, and explicitly against the lord pope."[41] The commune and the canon acknowl-

---

40. Greenaway, *Arnold*, 123. Note 3 is the Latin text of the rescript.
41. John of Salisbury, *Historia Pontificalis*, 61. Appendix, I. A., 127.

edged that they stood together. The City continued its self-rule and clergy who remained loyal to Arnold rebelled against the pope in doing so, though not against the Catholic Christian faith.

Greenaway characterized this pact as "a purely defensive alliance based on political expediency designed to provide mutual safeguards against a papal *coup d' état*."[42] This may be accurate if one removes the word "purely," but it does not tell us enough about what this alliance intended. The alliance expressed a binding relationship between a congregation and a beloved prophet-pastor. Neither party felt coerced to enter this exchange of promises, and their compact was not broken by political or military pressure; in the end it was broken by religious pressure.

Most writers agree that this well-publicized excommunication and the resulting pact with the Senate launched Arnold into a new phase of his career. Although he did not cross the line to join in governance, he continued to champion self-determination for the City. However, from this time forward his preaching and teaching appear to have become more explicit, with clear political implications. We shall return to this shortly.

Meanwhile, the pope left Brescia for Viterbo, a city with which Rome was at war.[43] In April 1149, he moved from Viterbo to Tusculum, intending to organize an assault on Rome.

> Eugenius, who had brought the necessary money with him from France, collected the vassals of the Church and reinforcements of mercenaries in Tusculum, placed Cardinal Guido of Puella at the head of these troops, and in his distress formed an alliance with King Roger [of Sicily], who lent him soldiers. Rome was now reduced to the uttermost extremity, but the republicans valiantly repulsed the attacks of the enemy.[44]

Bernard of Clairvaux and Gerhoh of Reichersberg criticized Eugenius severely for this failed action. They objected to the pope resorting to weapons of war. Bernard wrote: "Therefore, I say, attack them all the more, but with the word, not the sword. Why should you try to usurp the sword anew which you were once commanded to sheathe?"[45] This is a bit odd, given the efforts of Bernard as well as Eugenius to promote the Second Crusade.

42. Greenaway, *Arnold*, 126.
43. Gregorovius, *Rome in the Middle Ages*, 508, 509.
44. Ibid., 509.
45. Bernard of Clairvaux, *On Consideration*, 117–119. With regard to Gerhoh, see Greenaway, 125.

Perhaps the outcome of the Crusade changed Bernard's thoughts about war. Or maybe he thought a crusade was different in that they had simply recruited soldiers to a cause, whereas in the assault on Rome, Pope Eugenius led the battle. The attack certainly reinforced the distance between Arnold and Eugenius and supports the thesis that it drew Arnold deeper into opposition to church politics and, consequently, a more forceful social and political critique.

The Letters of 1149

The Roman Senate pursued its policies by sending letters to King Conrad urging him to receive the imperial crown from Rome. They wrote Conrad in 1149, before November, when Eugenius attacked the City with armed force. The Senators were aware the pope was preparing to attack them. The letter reads:

> [O]ur unanimous endeavour that we may again restore the empire of the Romans, which God has entrusted to your guidance, to the might that it possessed under Constantine and Justinian, who, empowered by the Roman Senate and people, governed the world.
> We have, therefore, by the help of God, restored the Senate, and defeated many enemies of your imperial rule, in order that what belonged to Caesar should be yours. We have laid a solid foundation. We are security for justice and peace to all such as shall desire them. We have conquered the fortresses of the civic nobility, who, supported by Sicily and by Pope Eugenius, hoped to defy you, and have either held these towns for you or have destroyed them.
> We are, therefore, harried on every side by the Pope, the Frangipani, the sons of Pierleone (with the exception of Jordan our standard-bearer), by Ptolemy, and by many others. They desire to prevent our crowning you Emperor.
> Meanwhile we suffer much hardship out of love to you, since there is nothing too hard for those who love, and you will give us the recompense due from a father, and merited punishment to the enemies of the empire. Shut your ears to the slanderers of the Senate; they will rejoice at our discord, in order to ruin you and us. Remember how much harm the papal court and these our former fellow-citizens [the Frangipani, etc.] have caused your predecessors, and how, with Sicilian aid, they have sought to do still further harm to the city.

Nevertheless, with Christ's help we hold out manfully for you, and we have already driven several of the empire's worst enemies out of the city. Hasten to our aid with imperial power; the city is at your command. You can dwell in Rome, the Capital of the world, and, more absolute than almost any of your predecessors, after every priestly obstacle is removed, can rule over the whole of Italy and the German empire.

We entreat you do not delay. Deign to assure your willing servants of your well-being by letters and messengers. We are now actively occupied in restoring the Milvian Bridge, which to the misfortune of the emperors has long been destroyed, and we hope soon to complete it with strong masonry. Your army will therefore be able to cross it, and to surround S. Angelo, where the Pierleoni, according to arrangement with Sicily [King Roger] and the Pope, meditate your ruin.[46]

The senators had thought things through; they expressed themselves sincerely with a pretty good political campaign position paper. Some scholars say this letter is too crude for Arnold to have had a hand in. He may not have participated, but that it is "crude" eludes me; it is clear in expression and intent. The charge of crudeness is not made of a second letter written the same year by an unnamed "faithful adherent of the Senate."[47] Shorter and well-written, Giesebrecht concluded Arnold was its author. Greenaway states, "Certainly this interpretation would fit Arnold's case, bound to the Senate as he was by the strongest of ties."[48]

Citing the case of Gregory I, the letter argued that the emperor should have the right to veto a papal election. The writer urged Conrad to come quickly to Rome and regulate the affairs of the City and limit ecclesiastical authority. He concluded, "For it is not the priest's function to bear both the sword and the chalice, but to preach the word of God, to confirm his teaching by good works, and by no means to stir up wars and strife throughout the world."[49] Arnold's message in a nutshell.

Benson observes that these letters of 1149 were respectful of the king. The "senatorial spokesmen did not consider the coronation constitutive

---

46. Roman Senate, Wibaldi epistolae, 214:332–334. Quotation translated by Annie Hamilton in Gregorovius, 512, 513.

47. Ibid., Wibald, 216:235, 236. Letters 214, 215, and 216 are considered the three letters of 1149. See also Benson, 342–346.

48. Greenaway, 130.

49. Roman Senate, Wibald, Ep. 216, Jaffe, 336 and Greenaway, 131.

with respect to anything other than the imperial title: after the coronation, Conrad would be rightly entitled *imperator Romanorum*, and would govern as emperor what had already been rightly his as *rex Romanorum*." But, "by envisioning the creation of an emperor as a secular act—that is, without an anointment and without the active collaboration of the papacy—the Romans perceived correctly, and attempted to revive, a central feature of constitutional procedure in late Antiquity."[50]

Conrad did not respond favorably to the Roman proposal. For one thing, he accepted the counsel of his advisor, Abbot Wibald of Stablo and Corvey (1098–1158). Wibald, in whose letter collection we find these letters from the Romans, was a staunch supporter of the papacy.[51] Pope Eugenius corresponded with Wibald regularly, asking him to exert his influence on the emperor, which he did.

Conrad wrote back in September of 1151, addressing his reply to "the Prefect of the city; the consuls, the captains and the whole Roman people." He does not seem to have seriously considered shifting from an ecclesiastical to a secular coronation. He wrote the letter to Rome, but he ignored the Senate. He promised to come to Italy to establish peace when he had recovered from his expedition to the Holy Land.[52] Conrad's promised visit never took place because he died in February, 1152.

Meanwhile, Pope Eugenius, in spite of military failure, gained residence in the City in November of 1149. He was unable, however, to establish effective control or dislodge Arnold from his position as ecclesiastical leader. In fact, whether because Arnold and the Arnoldists—the sect of the Lombards—became stronger and more outspoken, or because the pope's relation with the Senate and the people in general was unsustainable, or both, by June, 1150, Eugenius left the city and returned to Latium, residing in Segni and sometimes in Ferentino until the fall of 1152.

During this time, Arnold became increasingly active preaching and teaching his doctrine of separation of church and state and the proper relationship between the sacred and secular. The letter to Conrad from a "faithful adherent of the Senate" had stated clearly that ministers of the church have no role in matters of the sword and that *dominium temporale* does not belong to the church. John of Salisbury summarized Arnold's message as follows:

50. Benson, "Political *Renovatio*," 346.
51. See Gregorovius, 515 and Greenaway, 131–134.
52. Conrad III, Letter to Rome, Wibald, Ep. 345, Jaffe, 479.

> [T]he Pope himself was not what he professed to be—an apostolic man and shepherd of souls—but a man of blood who maintained his authority by fire and sword, a tormentor of churches and oppressor of the innocent... so far from apostolic that he imitated neither the life nor the doctrine of the apostles, wherefore neither obedience nor reverence was due to him: and in any case no man could be admitted who wished to impose a yoke of servitude on Rome, the seat of Empire, fountain of liberty and mistress of the world.[53]

Wezel's Letter to Frederick Barbarossa

The letters of 1149 continued to recognize the right of the German king to the imperial throne. In these letters, the Senate claimed the authority to crown the king belonged to it—the Roman Senate, *not* the pope. In a letter written in 1152 to Conrad's successor, Frederick Barbarossa, the otherwise unknown Wezel[54] introduced an argument providing foundation for the claim that right of election belongs to the Roman people. This marked a new development in the conversation, and, if Wezel's thought was shared by the Senate, indicated a new development in its political philosophy as well.

Perhaps the letter was written in collaboration with Arnold. Arnold was *persona non grata* among popes and kings; withholding his name, if he participated, was prudent. The matter of Wezel's and, likely, Arnold's purpose must be considered before proceeding.

The Wezel letter has generally been treated as a political document that expressed the more radical thinking of a party within the Senate and among the people of Rome. Although it *might* have represented the view of a radical faction and though it *has been taken* as a political document, it *was* a *pastoral letter* to the new king.[55] It contained a clear, biblically sup-

---

53. John of Salisbury, *Historia Pontificalis*, 65, Appendix I.A., 120.

54. There are two main theories about Wezel's identity. First theory: "Wetzel [alternative spelling] was undoubtedly a German, and had probably come to Rome with Arnold." Gregorovius, 519, n. 1. Alfieri seems to concur: "Some German men attached themselves to him and then followed him on his return to Italy," 594. Second theory: the name is a pseudonym for Arnold. This hypothesis is advanced by Hampe and considered quite possible by Greenaway. See Greenaway, 137, 138. In either case, Gregorovius and Alfieri agree that the letter accurately represents Arnold's position at the time.

55. Wezel, Letter, Ep. inter Wibald, Ep. 404, Jaffe, 539–543. Because of the importance of this letter, a translation by Mary Preuss is printed in Appendix. I. F., 140–144.

ported description of the calling of the Apostle Peter and his successors, and it spelled out the proper role of clergy and church. Related to this, and largely derived from it, the writer described the origins of secular authority. He advised the young king as to the true understanding of life, warned him against the pope—who was not the vicar of Christ—and his clergy, instructed the king on how to establish his government on a proper foundation, and how to fulfill his calling, if he was properly called, for the benefit of the empire and of his own soul. It was a bold letter.

Wezel based his counsel on his convictions and valid reasoning, providing scriptural and secular authority as precedents. The letter is personal and its purpose pastoral, similar to Bernard's when he wrote *On Consideration* to Eugenius III.

The content is consistent with Arnold's preaching, with his reputation as a person of learning and student of Scripture, and echoes Arnold's pastoral evangelical boldness, all of which supports the notion that the letter reflects Arnold's influence, and, perhaps, his direct participation.

Beyond its pastoral content, the letter dealt with three major matters: the role of Rome, the role of law, and the role of the church as each bears on establishing the secular realm. Wezel was happy Frederick was elected king, but unhappy that the king had not consulted the mother and creator of rulers, the holy City of Rome.

He used the biblical story of Jacob and Esau to make his point. Jacob received Isaac's blessing by following the advice of his mother, Rebecca, who made the choice between Jacob and his brother, Esau. He admonished Frederick to look to Rome, his mother, as Jacob looked to Rebecca. He should not have made the mistake of looking to the pope, as Esau looked to his father.

Wezel relied on Scripture and church history to demonstrate that crowning kings and ruling people is *not* the role of the servants of Christ. Apostle Peter understood this and did not at any time insert himself in civic affairs. There was a marked contrast between what Peter taught and the lives and claims of the contemporary pope and cardinals. It is not difficult, he believed, to see that Peter's description of false teachers applied to the pope, the cardinals, and other powerful clergy. "There will be false teachers (II Peter 2:1), and in their greed they will exploit you with false words (2:3), reveling in their dissipation, carousing with you (2:13). They have eyes full of adultery (2:14), and because of them the way of truth will be reviled (2:2), these are waterless springs and mists driven by a storm (2:17)."

How could the papacy honestly claim, "Lo, we have left all and followed you" (Matt. 19:27)? or "Silver and gold have I none" (Acts 3:6)? Wesel could hardly have framed the issue more strikingly. It brings to mind John of Salisbury and others who said that Arnold was an outstanding scholar and teacher of Scripture.

The writer argued that true use of history and tradition does *not* support the false claims of the papacy. In light of Scripture, the riches of the clergy are self-incriminating and further, he wrote: quoting Jerome, "Flee the clerical business man, either one who has become rich out of poverty or one who has become famous out of obscurity, flee him like the plague."

He next cited the Pseudo-Isidorian writing in which Peter commands Clement to stay out of secular business: "For if you get occupied with worldly cares, you deceive both yourself and those who hear you . . . the result will be that you will be put down from office and that your students will perish through ignorance. Therefore, leave yourself free for this alone, that you teach the word of God without ceasing."

Wezel brought up the Donation of Constantine to further convince King Frederick that the church under the popes was in the wrong. The document by which popes had long supported their claims to temporal authority, he wrote, is false. "In truth that lie and heretical fable in which it is related that Constantine yielded imperial authority to Sylvester, by simony, was so well known in the city that even mercenaries and poor women argued with people as learned as you please about it."[56]

Wezel claimed the rule of law and the authority of the Roman people as the *genuine* foundation of the empire. Once again he used the example of Esau and Jacob. Jacob snatched his father's blessing with divine assent, and followed his mother's instructions, by covering neck and hands with something analogous to law, the "household covering of teaching."

The pastoral letter continued, demonstrating a breadth of learning, by quoting a basic principle from Justinian: "The authority of imperial rule ought to be adorned and armed not only by weapons, but also by laws. So that in either a time of war or a time of peace, it is governed properly."

This led to the conclusion, also based upon Justinian, that the emperor had the power to make laws and benefit from them because the Roman people yielded the authority to him. But it all comes from the Roman people. What

---

56. For the text of the Donation of Constantine see Henry Bettenson, *Documents of the Christian Church*, 137–142 or http://legacy.fordham.edu/Halsall/source/donatconst.asp

had been overlooked in discussions to date, Wezel observed, was: "What law or reason prevents the Senate and people from creating an emperor?"

In the closing paragraph he indicated his sincerity and the sincerity of the people of Rome in wanting to work with Frederick. He asked the king to send ambassadors who understand and dare to discuss the law, namely the three men from the diocese of Constance, Rudulf, Ulrich, and Eberhard, whom we encountered earlier, men with whom Arnold had established good relationships in Zurich. In addition, Wezel warned the king to watch out for himself and be on guard against rebellion in his own court.[57]

Arnold's Position

Arnold understood society in light of the Gospels and the earlier church. He accepted secular government as proper and the mission of the church as caring for souls and promoting the Gospel—not to ruling, running governments, gaining wealth and power, nor, heaven forbid, fighting wars.

When it came to government, one suspects that his experience with the people of Brescia, his belief in their legitimate right to govern, and his classical education, inspired by Abelard's love of Greek philosophy and the history of the democratic cities of ancient Greece shaped his convictions. The democratic practices and literature of Rome, inclined him to reject top-down theories of papal, church, or imperial authority. Authority arose from the people—first of all the people of Rome.

What gave the people of Rome authority? First, it was granted through the facts and circumstances of history. Rome was chosen by providence. It was chosen in secular matters as Israel was chosen in spiritual matters. Later Frederick contended that the Germans had succeeded Rome in that respect.[58] Arnold was not willing to accept that comparison, but he would have pushed the point, implicit in Frederick's statement, that secular power was *ordained separately* from ecclesiastical power. Second, the people of Rome represented people everywhere.

---

57. Wezel, Letter, Ep. inter Wibald, Ep. 404, Jaffe, 539–543

58. Otto, *Deeds*, 146–149. See "Crowning the Emperor" in chapter 6 for part of the text and a summary of Frederick's response to the Roman envoys.

Pope Eugenius's Letter to Wibald

Another letter, dated September 20, 1152, made its way to Germany about the same time. Pope Eugenius wrote to Wibald,[59] the influential abbot of Stablo and Corvey, relating his troubles with the people of Rome, claiming knowledge of a plan of some 2,000 radicals—the *rusticana turba* led by Arnold—to take control of the Senate on November 1, 1152.

According to the pope, the "radicals" wanted to create 100 senators and two consuls. One of the consuls would have authority within the city and the other outside the city ("reflecting" writes Benson, "the division of responsibility between the ancient *praetores urbanus* and *peregrinus*"). The consul for those outside the city is the "one whom they want to call emperor." Eugenius urged Wibald to secretly inform Frederick of these developments so that the king could take appropriate action. Benson's summary is concise:

> If this papal account is accurate, Arnold and a group of poorer and less eminent Romans had taken control of the communal movement in 1152. In all likelihood, they anticipated—correctly—that the new German King would refuse their crown and their offer of a Roman alliance; hence the decision to elect an emperor soon and, undoubtedly, to choose one of the commune's leaders as emperor. By assuming that the German king had no inherent claim on the imperial office, Wesel expressed a central conviction of this new group: the Roman people are free to elect as emperor whomever they wish. In any case, the episode was brief, cooler heads seem to have prevailed, and the election planned for November 1, 1152 evidently never took place.[60]

Caution is advised in relying upon the pope's words and Benson's conclusions in this matter. "If this papal account is accurate" begins Benson—*if*. Clearly Eugenius had a motive for sounding an alarm that he hoped would bring action from the King. Further, the use of the term "cooler" heads by Benson suggests an interpretation not necessarily warranted—especially since there is no other word about this matter except the pope's supposed intelligence. Eugenius may well have heard a rumor that both scared him and also made good propaganda, but there may actually have been few, if

---

59. Eugenius, Letter, Ep. inter Wibald 403, Jaffe, 537–539. For interpretations of this letter and accounts of the events related to it, see Gregorovius, 521, Greenaway, 142–144, and Benson, 349, 350.

60. Benson, "Political *Renovatio*," 346.

any, *hot* heads and if there were, identifying Arnold as leader added alarm to the rumor. The promised event did not happen, nor did Rome cease its efforts to persuade Frederick to accept the crown from the City. They kept trying to win Frederick over right up to the last moment—April of 1155.

Eugenius's letter, however, may have spurred the king to enter into the Treaty of Constance with the pope, which he did in March of 1153. By treaty, Frederick promised to undertake the recovery and defense of the pope's temporal power and the pope promised to crown Frederick emperor in Rome and to uphold his authority as best he could.[61]

Prior to this, on December 9, 1152, Pope Eugenius had reentered Rome. Greenaway reports that "[T]he senatorial elections resulted in the return of the moderate party by a large majority. By a liberal use of money [Eugenius] succeeded in winning over to his side all but the most fanatical of Arnold's adherents."[62] Eugenius did spread money around, but can we be sure "fanatical adherents" are not mainly an extension of a rumor? How readily do fanatical adherents succumb to money?

The pope and the Senate reached an agreement that included recognition of the commune, but it did not grant the pope authority to suppress Arnold and his people. They continued their pastoral care as their convictions dictated.

Pope Eugenius died at Tivoli on July 8, 1153. He was succeeded by Conrad, the cardinal bishop of Sabina, who took the name Anastasius IV. In his eighties when he became pope, Anastasius had a short reign; he died on December 3, 1154. He was a Roman by birth and reputed to be a peacemaker. It seems he did not focus on the subjugation of the commune as had Eugenius.

Adrian IV and the Exile of Arnold

Nicholas Breakspear, an English abbot whom Eugenius had named cardinal-bishop of Albano, succeeded Anastasius. On December 5, 1154, two months after returning from a legatine mission to Scandinavia, he was unanimously elected pope and took the name Adrian IV (or Hadrian). The first and (to date) only Englishman to become pope, he was tenacious and determined. The Senate refused to recognize him and he refused to recognize the Senate. He was dead set against Arnold and demanded that the

---

61. Ep. 407, inter Wibald Ep, Jaffe, 546, 547, is the text of the Treaty of Constance.
62. Greenaway, *Arnold*, 144.

Senate expel him. He set out to enlist Frederick to overthrow the republic, hoping thereby to solve both problems.

Adrian received no response from the Senate. Indeed, it appears that its resistance stiffened as Adrian persisted. Gregorovius writes, "With the overthrow of this one demagogue [Arnold], Adrian hoped to bury the republic, and the Romans, who had little to expect from Frederick, turned in secret to William I, who had succeeded his celebrated father Roger on the throne of Sicily in February 1145."[63]

The term demagogue, "a political leader who seeks support by appealing to popular desires and prejudices rather than by using rational argument," reflects a point of view, but does not accurately describe Arnold. Although he was a prophet, an apostle of liberty who influenced politics, and a thorn in the side of the papacy, it is not true that he was a political leader; furthermore, he was a champion of reason and rational debate. However, the ancient Greek and Roman meaning of demagogue, "a leader or orator who espoused the cause of the common people" does fit Arnold.

Adrian was unable to gain control of any part of the City, not even the Lateran Palace, which had been the papal residence from the fourth century, so he lived in fortified St. Peter's Basilica. Frederick Barbarossa, meanwhile, entered Italy. He attacked the Lombard cities that resisted him, careful, however, not to engage powerful Milan. Adrian waited, eager for the King's arrival; he needed his help badly.

Just at that moment, an unusual opportunity to rid Rome of Arnold presented itself. Enmity was riding high in the city toward the priests and clerics who were frustrating the goals of the Romans, and a cardinal, Guido of St. Pudentiana, was wounded—stabbed, on the Via Sacra while on his way to an audience with the pope. Adrian responded swiftly. He placed the City under an interdict—an ecclesiastical censure, unprecedented in the City of Rome.

The interdict meant that "the bare necessities of the spiritual life were all that were permitted. Children could be baptized and the confessions of the dying could be heard; but the churches were closed, and there could be no mass, no communion, no confirmation, no solemnization of marriage, no Extreme Unction."[64]

It was Holy Week, which greatly heightened the interdict's impact. The people were stunned and afraid. The usually brisk tourist business of Holy

---

63. Gregorovius, *Rome in the Middle Ages*, 526.
64. Mann, *The English Pope*, 23.

Week diminished to virtually nothing. Gregorovius described the interdict as "a species of moral starvation."[65] He observed that in later years, after the interdict had been frequently and widely applied, its power dissipated. But before 1155, it had not been used extensively and had never been imposed upon Rome; consequently, it was extremely effective. The Romans held out until Wednesday. They pleaded with Adrian, who agreed to lift the interdict *if* the senators would banish Arnold. The Senate yielded, sent Arnold away, and the interdict was lifted.

After nearly nine years, Arnold was on the move again. What did he think now? What were his hopes and plans? To whom could he turn? Did his faith and his vision of the way of Jesus continue to sustain him? This was the most sudden of his banishments, and he was immediately a renegade. He fled north, was captured by Cardinal Odo of St. Nicholas at Bricole in the valley of the Orcia, and imprisoned in a monastery of the Camaldulenses. The Viscounts of Campagnatico rescued him and hospitably provided shelter and respect.[66]

Meanwhile, "on Maundy Thursday (March 23, 1155), amidst a great crowd of rejoicing people, Adrian, surrounded by his cardinals, went in solemn procession from the Leonine city to the Lateran. There he celebrated the festival of Easter in the usual joyous fashion."[67]

Summary

The duration of the compact between Arnold and Rome (1149–1155), following, as it did, three years of Arnold's pastoral services in the city prior to 1149, testifies to the quality and significance of Arnold's ministry. He drew about him those willing to take up an ascetic life and devote themselves to pastoral care. The contributions of the canons regular, the lower clergy, and dedicated lay people served the commune of Rome well. Had they not, the compact would not have persisted. Beyond this, Arnold had both the knowledge and power of interpretation to provide the Senate with philosophical, historical, and theological foundation for its existence and purpose.

Greenaway wrote of the "ignorance" of the authors of the Roman constitution.[68] We must remember the general level of education in Europe

---

65. Gregorovius, *Rome in the Middle Ages*, 527.
66. See Gregorovius, 528, Greenaway, 151, and Davison, 157.
67. Mann, *The English Pope*, 24.
68. Greenaway, *Arnold*, 116.

was limited at the time, though a revival of learning was underway. The people of Rome were probably no more ignorant than others. There were few books available to them about the past—all the more reason Arnold was important to the Senate. He knew the glory of the story of Rome. Like other scholars of his time, he had memorized many passages from the ancients. He taught the Romans and helped them understand their civic life in light of historical precedent.[69]

Important as they were, the arguments from historical precedent interested Arnold secondarily. He believed the real justification for faith, action, and order was in Scripture—especially with respect to the fundamental matter of understanding church and ministry. Scripture made clear what it meant to respond to a religious calling—the proper role of monk, canon, priest, bishop, and pope was to live a life of service that included renunciation of worldly ambitions.

It was clear to him that the Senate, elected by the people, was the legitimate ruler of the City's civil life and that the Christian minister had no place in secular rule—except possibly as a substitute when no one else was available. For instance, the popes—the Bishops of Rome—had stepped into the power vacuum in the West when the Roman emperors moved to Constantinople. In this respect, the church had provided valuable service because popes and bishops kept order in western Europe, and monks and nuns kept learning alive.

Did Arnold recognize the value of the church's interim help in secular affairs? Likely he did. A few observers portrayed him as a narrow minded rabble-rouser unable to see other points of view. Not likely. Arnold and Abelard had engaged in stimulating conversations in which they reflected upon complex issues, including the structure of society. John of Salisbury said that Arnold was keen of intellect and John, himself a student of Abelard, knew that meant engaged, honest thinking.

If there had been appropriate, *ad hoc* governance by the pope in the West, its time was long past. Now, a people had arisen, revived by the consciousness that they were the Roman Republic, ready for secular rule. This was a new time, a time of spiritual revival, a time of re-formation, and Arnold was its spiritual and intellectual leader. It was time for the church

---

69. One might suggest and support the thought that in this respect Arnold understood something Friedrich Nietzsche expressed later—the importance of history and the use or advantage of it is determined by what is most urgent or necessary in the present. His exact words were: "You can explain the past only by what is most powerful in the present." Friedrich Nietzsche, *The Use and Abuse of History*, 40.

to relinquish its rule now that communes throughout Italy and all Europe were properly taking hold of governments, and a revived Roman Senate was ready once again to take up its task of crowning the emperor.

Arnold's compact with the Senate survived every assault until, ironically, it was broken by religious power, proving, ironically, Arnold's contention that the genuine power of the church was spiritual. The papacy, unable to prevail by secular power, finally succeeded when it brought the full weight of its religious power to bear—when by its own initiative, via the interdict, put the spiritual welfare of the people of Rome up against the life of one man and made the people choose.

6

Martyr

Excitement with apprehension was high throughout Italy. Pope Adrian and his cardinals waited nervously for the arrival of the young, powerful German, Frederick "Red beard." After a siege lasting two months, Frederick's army laid waste the town of Tortona, and on April 17, he received the Iron Crown of Lombardy at Pavia. Reports of Frederick's ruthless actions in the north worried Adrian.

The pope met with his cardinals, Peter, the Prefect of Rome, and Odo Frangipane, a consul, at Sutri. They decided to send three cardinals—one of them Guido of St. Pudentiana, recovered from his wounds—to meet Frederick. To test the king's good will, they asked him to deliver Arnold of Brescia to them. Frederick responded to this request without delay. He sent troops to the fortress of the Viscounts of Campagnatico where Arnold was residing, captured one of the counts, held him hostage, and offered him for Arnold. The exchange was made; the Brescian was placed under arrest and turned over to the pope's Prefect.[1]

Crowning the Emperor

The pope was not the only person anxious about Frederick's arrival. The people of Rome were worried, too. If unable to persuade the prince to align

---

1. The primary source for these events is Otto of Freising, *Deeds*, 142–153. The secondary accounts we rely upon are Mann, *The English Pope*, 16–41; Gregorovius, *Rome in the Middle Ages*, 524–550; Balzani, *The Popes and the Hohenstaufen* 29–40; and Greenaway, *Arnold*, 147–163.

himself with them, the commune faced the prospect of a bloody battle against Frederick's great army *and* the pope's troops. News of Frederick's activities in the north did not engender calm. The Senate arranged to send a delegation to meet Frederick and make Rome's case.

Although the Romans may have missed Arnold's counsel, they were probably relieved that he was no longer a bone of contention.

As Frederick approached Viterbo, the pope and king sent ambassadors to one another. Both resolved not to accept the ambassadors of the other until their own representatives had returned—a logically impossible situation. Fearful, Adrian moved from Viterbo to Civita Castellana for safety.[2]

As they returned to their respective leaders, the two embassies encountered one another and agreed to proceed to Frederick's camp near Viterbo. Upon their arrival, Frederick swore before the pope's representatives and his own properly constituted court that he would not harm the pope nor any of his retinue, nor allow any aggression against the pope's honor or possessions.[3]

Thus assured, Pope Adrian went to Nepi and Frederick moved his camp to Campo Grasso near Sutri. On June 9, Adrian and his cardinals rode to the German camp. The initial reception was friendly, but when Frederick did not come forward as groom to hold the pope's stirrup while he dismounted—a traditional mark of respect[4]—the cardinals turned their horses and fled to Civita Castellana. Abandoned, Adrian took the seat prepared for him.

Frederick approached to kiss the pope's feet and to exchange the kiss of peace. Adrian drew back saying that he would not give the kiss of peace unless the king first showed him the respect that Frederick's predecessors had shown. Frederick said it was not his duty to be the pope's groom. Adrian refused to proceed unless Frederick complied, and returned to his camp. One wonders what the pope said to the cardinals who abandoned him.

---

2. For those who have access to google maps, using Rome as the entry, one can view a map of the territory between Rome and Viterbo where these activities took place.

3. Mann, *The English Pope*, 30.

4. The practice was based on the statement in the the Donation of Constantine, http://legacy.fordham.edu/halsall/source/donatconst.asp. "And, holding the bridle of his horse, out of reverence for St. Peter we [Constantine] performed for him [Pope Sylvester] the duty of groom." "Bridle" has become stirrup by the time of Frederick; the intention is the same. It is interesting that in Wezel's letter to Frederick of 1152, he stated that the Donation was a forgery—obvious to the common people of Rome, not just scholars. Yet, it is not until 1440 that Lorenzo Valla is credited with proving it a forgery.

Frederick's advisors convinced him "by the testimony of the older princes, and by the records of history, that precedent was against [him], and it was decided that, 'out of reverence for the blessed Apostles,' he should perform the office of groom to the Pope."[5]

The Germans moved camp to Lake Janula (now Lake Monterosi) near Monterosi. When Adrian arrived on June 11, "the mighty Emperor performed the part of groom to the Vicar of Christ, walked at the distance of a stone's throw beside the palfrey of the former beggar of S. Albans, and vigorously adjusted his stirrup."[6] "The kiss of peace then given by the pope sealed the reconciliation of these two iron characters."[7]

They proceeded together toward Rome and on the way met the Roman envoys who had been granted safe passage. This was a story for Shakespeare. The Romans stated their case emphatically.

> "We the ambassadors of the City ... O Excellent King, have been sent to Your Excellency by the senate and people of Rome ... You seek authority over the world; I arise willingly to give you the crown ... You were a stranger. I made you a citizen. You were a newcomer from the regions beyond the Alps. I have established you as prince. What was rightfully mine I gave to you. You ought therefore first afford security for the maintenance of my good customs and ancient laws ... To my officials, who must acclaim you on the Capitol, you should give as much as five thousand pounds as expense money. You should avert harm from the republic even to the extent of the shedding of your blood, and safeguard all this by privileges, and establish it by the interposition of an oath with your own hand."
>
> Hereupon the king, inflamed with righteous anger by the tenor of a speech as insolent as it was unusual, interrupted ... as [the Romans] were about to spin out their oration in the Italian fashion by lengthy and circuitous periods. Preserving his royal dignity with modest bearing and charm of expression he replied without preparation but not unprepared.
>
> "We have heard much heretofore concerning the wisdom and the valor of the Romans, yet more concerning their wisdom. Wherefore we cannot wonder enough at finding your words

---

5. Mann, *The English Pope*, 31. See also note 1 in which Mann discusses Gregorovius's point of view as expressed in the latter's work, 531, 532.

6. Gregorovius, *Rome in the Middle Ages*, 531. Adrian, Nicholas Breakspear, was raised in close connection with the monastery of St. Albans in England where his father had become a monk in later life. Greenaway, *Arnold*, 148.

7. Mann, *The English Pope*, 32.

insipid with swollen pride rather than seasoned with the salt of wisdom. You set forth the ancient renown of your city. You extol to the very stars the ancient status of your sacred republic. Granted, granted! To use the words of your own writer, 'There was, *there was once* [emphasis in text] virtue in this republic.' 'Once,' I say. And O that we might truthfully and freely say 'now!' Your Rome—nay, ours also—has experienced the vicissitudes of time. She could not be the only one to escape a fate ordained by the Author of all things for all that dwell beneath the orb of the moon."[8]

Frederick continued, speaking longer than the Romans. He responded point by point to their assertions and demands. What was in Rome, he asserted, now belonged to the Franks. "Not yet has the hand of the Franks or the Germans been made weak." There was no reason he should take an oath to observe the laws since it was under willingness to protect the laws and the fatherland that he had become king. And, "that I should personally swear to pay you a certain sum of money. How disgraceful!"[9]

Otto concluded his account:

> With these words, and not without a justifiable indignation of spirit, he brought his speech to an end and was silent.
>
> And when certain of the bystanders inquired of the ambassadors whether they wished to say anything more, after deliberating a little they deceitfully replied that they wished first to report to their fellow citizens the things which they had heard, and return to the prince only after taking counsel.[10]

Frederick, in consultation with Adrian, dispatched about a thousand men to occupy St. Peter's. The next morning, June 18, 1155, Pope Adrian placed the imperial crown of Holy Roman Emperor on the head of Frederick I.

After the pope said, "Receive this emblem of glory in the name of the Father and of the Son and of the Holy Ghost, and so wear it in justice and mercy that you may receive from our Lord the crown of eternal life," the

---

8. Otto, *Deeds*, 143–149. The address by the Romans, 145, 146, and Frederick's responde, 146–149. For the full text of the speech of the Romans' and a partial text of Frederick's speech, see Appendix I.G., 144–146. It is hard to imagine a speech more unlikely to obtain its objective than that of the Romans.

9. Ibid., 148.

10. Ibid., 149.

Germans raised a tremendous cheer—a cheer which according to Cardinal Boso seemed like a thunderbolt had suddenly fallen from heaven.[11]

When the Romans learned about the coronation, they assembled and, in the early afternoon, rushed across the bridges into the Leonine City. It was clear Frederick and Adrian were their enemies and they attacked them without hesitation. Gregorovius comments, "Their courageous conduct showed that the constitution of the republic was not altogether a fantastic whim."[12]

Perhaps as many as 1000 Romans were slain or drowned in the Tiber trying to capture the bridges to the Vatican, and about 200 were taken prisoner. In spite of these losses the Romans continued to defend the City. Frederick abandoned the idea of taking Rome and, on the morning of the nineteenth, broke camp. He took the pope and all his cardinals and marched toward Tivoli, destroying the towers the Roman nobles had erected upon their estates. Thus, the emperor left Rome *without* having delivered it to the pope, and began making his warring way out of Italy.

Arnold's Final Witness

We do not know for sure where or when or under whose direct auspices, Arnold was executed. We know he was tried, condemned, and hanged. After he died, his body was burned and his ashes thrown into the Tiber River, leaving no relics for his followers to venerate.

Gregorovius, acknowledging that the scene of the execution was uncertain, thought it likely Arnold was executed on the 19th of June in the neighborhood of Soracte, a mountain just north of the City, while Frederick, his army, and the pope, were retreating from Rome.[13]

> After his surrender he was handed over to the City Prefect, who with his powerful family owned large estates in the county of Viterbo. They had long made war on the Roman commune, had suffered severe injuries at its hands, and consequently cherished feelings of bitter indignation against Arnold. After he had been condemned by a spiritual tribunal the Prefect sentenced him (and undoubtedly with the Emperor's sanction) to death as a heretic and a rebel.[14]

---

11. Mann, *The English Pope*, 36.
12. Gregorovius, *Rome in the Middle Ages*, 542.
13. Ibid., 544.
14. Ibid., 542

Martyr

In 1887, Ernesto Monaci published *Gesta di federico primi in Italia* containing a long poem about Frederick's coronation campaign of 1155. This poem, written by an eye-witness to Arnold's hanging, shed new light on him and his death.[15] The poet from Bergamo, known as the Bergamese Poet, disapproved of Arnold just as Otto and Bernard did, but when he began to describe the canon's death, his tone changed. Arnold did not act as the Poet expected. Perhaps he expected Arnold to crack under pressure or harangue his executioners with words of damnation. He did neither; he addressed his standing before God.

> But when he saw that his punishment was prepared, and that his neck was to be bound in the halter by hurrying fate, and when he was asked if he would renounce his false doctrine, and confess his sins after the manner of the wise, fearless and self-confident, wonderful to relate, he replied that his own doctrine seemed to him sound, nor would he hesitate to undergo death for his teachings, in which there was nothing absurd or dangerous.
>
> And he requested a short delay for time to pray, for he said that he wished to confess his sins to Christ. Then on bended knees, with eyes and hands raised up to heaven, he groaned, sighing from the depths of his breast, and silently communed in spirit with God, commending to Him his soul. And after a short time, prepared to suffer with constancy, he surrendered his body to death.
>
> Those who looked on at his punishment shed tears; even the executioners were moved by pity for a little time, while he hung from the noose which held him. And it is said that the king, moved too late by compassion, mourned over this.[16]

In this account, we are close to a direct quote from Arnold. It requires only slight modification to make it so, and to hear, at last, the words of Arnold himself.

Official of the execution: "Will you renounce your false doctrine and confess your sins?"

Arnold: "My doctrine seems sound to me. I will not hesitate to undergo death for my teachings for there is nothing absurd or dangerous in them. I would like a brief delay, however, for I wish to confess my sins to Christ."

His request was granted and "then on bended knees ... he groaned and sighing from his breast, he silently communed in spirit with God." It was

---

15. The discovery of *Gesta di Federico* provided information about Arnold that required revision of his history. The translation does not attempt to be poetic.

16. The Bergamese Poet, "Frederick in Italy," in *The Portable Medieval Reader*, 343; and Appendix I.D, 137-139.

clear to the Poet and onlookers that Arnold prayed with integrity, which threw new light on his life and ministry for those who had not known him in person; most only knew the reputation that they had learned from his enemies. The impact of Arnold's death upon the onlookers indicates that the living presence and spirit of this courageous reformer and champion of liberty was much different from the reputation ascribed to him by those who opposed and feared him.

The Poet's Questions

The Poet from Bergamo posed these questions for Arnold: "Learned Arnold, what did such great learning profit you, and so much fasting, and so many labours? Of what profit was such a hard life, which spurned all slothful leisure and enjoyed no fleshly pleasures?"[17]

Because these questions were asked personally, they deserve to be considered personally—questions Arnold, like many contemporaries, would have little difficulty answering. Bernard of Clairvaux and his Cistercian brothers and Arnold and his fellow canons would answer that their sacrifices were worth everything. Arnold's life from that perspective was extremely "profitable;" a life without learning and dedication unprofitable. He was free of, and preached that all clergy could and should be free of the entanglements of secular power. Without what the Poet called "sacrifices," he would not have known Peter Abelard, taught in Paris and Zurich, nor participated in one of the most distinctive political movements of the time, one that has continued to have impact into our own time.

The Poet's next question was more specific. "Alas, what made you turn your biting slander upon the Church so that you should come, O wretched one, to the sad noose?!" Was Arnold a slanderer? We have seen how his opposition to the papacy and rich clergy developed. Is the judgment of Horace Mann, which seems to reflect the judgment implicit in the Poet's question correct? Mann wrote:

> But it must be noted that [Arnold] was condemned not for desiring to reform the Church, nor for denouncing its corruptions, for he could not have done that more vigorously than Gerhoh of Reichersberg and Bernard of Clairvaux, but for sedition. There is one way of preaching a reformation of manners, which is that of men who are at once good and sensible, and which effects its purpose; there

17. Ibid.

> is another which leads to violence and bloodshed, and which is the way of the fool or of the rogue. "And it is only just to point out," writes Tarleton, "that, like all dreamers, Arnold was one-sided in his judgment; his enthusiasm only enabled him to see the abuse of riches in the Church, and failed to show him that she must, if she was to live, have the means necessary to carry out her mission, to keep up her dignity, to relieve her poorer members, and to maintain the worship of God; not to mention the training of her sons and the mission work of bringing fresh sheep to the fold."[18]

Arnold would likely reply: "I rejoice when the resources of the church are used rightly as my accuser describes; I support each of the purposes he lists. I bless all forms of human endeavor and ministry. But what do you mean, 'relieve her poorer members?' How much concern do the cardinals and bishops show for the poorer members? Ask the people. They will tell you of their experiences with the clergy. Have you heard the story on the street about St. Mark of Silver? Should we overlook the false claims of the papacy and deviations from Scripture?

"Besides, wealth is only half the problem; exercising secular power and obstructing self-rule of the communes with a system that must be abandoned in order for the church to be apostolic is at least as big a problem." Arnold was a reformer and also a forerunner of St. Francis.

Finally, the Poet exclaimed, "Behold your doctrine, O condemned one, for which you have paid the penalty! Doctrine passes away, and your teaching will not long survive! It has been burned and dissolved with you into a few ashes, lest perchance something might be left to be honoured."[19]

In response to this *and* to the judgments of Mann and Tarleton, let us turn to Gregorovius.

> Arnold of Brescia heads the series of celebrated martyrs for freedom who died upon the funeral pyre, but whose ardent genius rose like a phoenix from the flames to live through centuries. We might even call him a prophet, so clearly did he see into the spirit of his time, so far did he advance towards the goal, which, not until 700 years after him, Rome and Italy are hoping to reach.
>
> The already mature consciousness of his age was incarnate in the gifted person of the reformer, and the first political heretic of the Middle Ages, was the logical consequence of the quarrel for

---

18. Mann, *The English Pope*, 29. Tarleton is A. H. Tarleton, author of *Nicholas Breakspear, Englishman and Pope*.

19. The Bergamese Poet, "Frederick in Italy," 343.

investitures. The struggle of the two powers and the transformation of the cities were the great practical phenomena which served him as a historical basis.

An inner necessity drew him to the spot where the root of all the evil lay. If Arnold had not gone to Rome, had not ended his life here, he would have been an incomplete figure of his age. The constitution, to which Arnold may perhaps as a law-giver have largely contributed, nevertheless long survived him; the school of the Arnoldists . . . never died out. Arnold is the historic precedent for all the forces, theoretical or practical, which have revolted against the secular character of the clergy; this so much the more because his aims were not sullied by any sordid motives.

Arnold surpasses all his successors in the struggle for Roman liberty, not only in the greatness of his time, but also in the loftiness of his aims. Savanarola, with whom [Arnold] has been compared, is frequently rendered offensive to every manly judgment by the monastic character of his intellect and by his claims to supernatural powers. But neither miracles or oracles are attributed to the friend of Abelard. He seems to have been sane, manly, and clear . . . His teaching was of such enduring vitality, that it is still in harmony with the spirit of our time [1896], and Arnold of Brescia would now be the most popular man in Italy.[20]

Trail's End: Questions and Considerations

Arnold of Brescia died an honorable death in the presence of his enemies. What compelled his enemies to kill him? Was Arnold unrealistic as some say? Were he and the Roman Senate a pipe-dream in relation to the real political situation? There may be truth in yes answers. However, Arnold was focused on a *different kind* of realism. Frederick and Adrian were taken as realists. Frederic mocked the absurdity of poor, little, confused Rome claiming that it could make him emperor. Yet, can we say that the course he took, or the course of the papacy, was realistic and successful, without trouble or bloodshed?

Frederick's troubles with Italy—in particular with the Italian republics *and* the popes were just beginning. The king's ability and the pope's

---

20. Gregorovius, *Rome in the Middle Ages*, 547, 548. In note 1 on 548, Gregorovius reported, "On February 13, 1862, placards were posted in Loreto, on which was printed: *Viva il Papa no Re! Viva Arnolds da Brescia! Viva il Clero liberale!* In 1883 the city of Brescia erected a bronze statue to the famous reformer, to which Zurich also contributed."

authority to create an emperor had been severely tested. Frederick had to fight his way out of Italy. Pope Adrian did not fare much better; he was left without control of the City and a less than satisfactory ally in Frederick.

In the act of crowning Frederick as Holy Roman Emperor, dual authority was acknowledged without agreement as to who had higher authority. The City of Rome was not a player from either the imperial or papal point of view. However, neither pope nor king knew how to deal with communes and city republics. Throughout the centuries of struggle within the medieval system between church and emperor for supremacy, neither institution contemplated a third player.

Arnold thrust the third player, self-governing cities with independent populaces, at them both. He claimed the emperor should receive authority for his rule from the City of Rome, as if Rome were representative of all secular cities, and he wanted the church to stay entirely *out* of the business of secular rule. Neither church nor empire could envision the end , at least not an orderly end, of the medieval synthesis which assumed the unity of human life under one ultimate authority, God's authority as represented in the papacy. This unity was the papacy's prevailing view and thus shared by the bishops and the clergy. Arnold and his followers represented a threat that had to be done away with, and it was—for the time being. Yet, which view has turned out to have more lasting influence?

Arnold was a reformer just as several popes, monastic leaders, others before him, and many of his contemporaries were reformers. They, also, wanted to cleanse the church of corruption and excessive wealth. He went a step further than most by calling for complete separation of civil and ecclesiastical power; he saw separation of the two as an integral part of reform, just as Luther did. However, he did not share with Luther the decisively uncompromising theological conviction of salvation by faith alone. Further, although he had followers called Arnoldists, he did not propose to create a new separated church; he was not a proto-Protestant. Martin Luther King Jr is a better comparison as a reformer, prophet, and apostle of liberty.

The separation of the religious and the civil spheres threatened the undoing of the entire medieval synthesis. The unity of these spheres was the papacy's prevailing view and thus shared by the bishops and the clergy. They were unwilling to separate human affairs into two independent realms, church and state. Certainly there were historical-religious reasons for the rise of the medieval synthesis; it may have been the only solution for ordering society once the Roman Empire had fallen apart in the West.

As Arnold saw it, what had been the case should be the case no longer. Rome, and all it stood for, was back. The Senate and the Roman people (*Senatus Populusque Romanus*) minted coins.

Realization of historical reality helps one *understand* what had evolved in Western Europe, but it does not *justify* excesses and exploitation by church and clergy. A posture of "this is the way things are; this is the way the world is," generated perpetual cynicism and resistance to change.

Canons lived and worked among people in cities, in the heart of the developing economic and social order. No wonder, rooted as his life was in a religious order that was relatively faithful to its vows of simplicity and poverty, that the luxury and corruption of the Church earned Arnold's condemnation. It's difficult to understand how the ecclesiastical authorities were able to reconcile the church's wealth and power with the teachings and example of the New Testament.

The Renaissance of the twelfth century, like that of the fifteenth, was inspired by a renewed interest in antiquity— Greco-Roman and Christian. In the case of Arnold and Rome, reborn were a fresh desire for Latin literature, which stimulated intellectual exploration, and the idea that a city, in particular, Rome, should rule and be ruled as it had before Christianity became a social-political force.

Arnold was a scholar who believed in reason and loved learning. His brilliant teaching and preaching won adherents and followers on the one hand and, on the other, powerful opposition of both major institutions, especially the papacy, and their spokespersons. He taught in Paris, the center of the century's intellectual renaissance, and he was a careful reader of texts, both biblical and classical.

The order of canons regular was the framework in which Arnold fulfilled his role and played his position. He ate and slept in houses of the order which provided the foundation and fabric of his life and was the source of motivation for his actions—a fact that has been largely ignored in existing accounts and interpretations. Arnold was a canon regular, and it was as a canon regular, endorsed by the Senate, that he had the additional responsibility of presiding over the religious life of Rome. Arnold envisioned flourishing civil life created by the people as in the ancient Roman Republic and the Greek city-states.

According to Thomas Madden, the Romans of the Republic loved family and civil life above all else, eschewed empire, and took military action only to protect family life.[21] The Roman vision of family and civil life attracted Arnold. He read the Latin writers with enthusiasm, expanding his knowledge and deepening his understanding. He tasted and supported revival of civil life in the cities of Brescia, Paris, Zurich, and Rome. He was a student who embraced the liberal arts and diligently studied the *trivium*.

Arnold reminded all concerned that the civil life of Rome with its great writers and intelligent discourse owed nothing to the church. The Romans and the Greeks pursued values such as intelligent discourse, truth, friendship, and civic life centuries before the birth of Jesus. Furthermore, the followers of Jesus in the New Testament did not aspire to rule secular life on behalf of Jesus. What they owned, they owned in common. They devoted themselves to caring for their neighbors as they could. Their goal was to be kind and loving—to love their neighbors as themselves.

This was Arnold's vision of the true church—followers of Jesus supported by priests, nuns, monks, canons, and lay people seeking the good, lending a hand, listening to the sorrowing, embracing youth, praying, and studying; these were the ingredients, the fruits—of true reformation. As Christian people did these things, they were the living church. This is what Arnold preached and taught.

Whether one addressed the social change that Arnold envisioned from the point of view of the church or that of secular society, it ended in the same place—secular rule in socioeconomic affairs and an independent, giving, pastoral, servant church disentangled from secular rule.

Arnold was not a politician; he did not run any city. His pastoral role and his vows dictated that his work was religious. He made this boundary clear. Because the commune of Rome was convinced of his vision, knew his integrity, was impressed with his preaching and teaching, and grateful for the pastoral care provided by the canons and other religious, Arnold had the authority of the Senate to direct pastoral services for the populace. The Senate promised to protect him from interference from the pope. This was how things were in Rome from 1148 to 1155.

We've met remarkable people during this quest: John of Salisbury, Heloise, Peter the Venerable, Otto of Friesing, Peter Abelard, Cardinal Guido, Bishop Manfred, popes Innocent II, Eugenius III, and Adrian IV, Frederick Barbarossa, and Bernard of Clairvaux. Much of the life and spirit of the first half of the twelfth century can be seen through Arnold's life. He was among the leaders of this creative generation. Peter Abelard and two popes,

---

21. Thomas Madden, *Empires of Trust*, 38–62.

Celestine II and Celestine III, were friends. On the other side of the ledger he dealt with Innocent II, Bernard of Clairvaux, Eugenius III, and Adrian IV without giving quarter to any of them.

Arnold participated in the most significant constitutional development of the Middle Ages. Armed only with deeply held convictions—about human dignity, freedom of thought, the spiritual mission and temporal limitations of the church—he confronted the most powerful people and institutions in Europe. In the tradition of the great Hebrew prophets, he spoke forth with authority against the injustice caused by the wealth and the temporal power of the church. When he was martyred for his devotion to these convictions, he accepted it with grace. Arnold's life and death indicated for future generations the depth of his commitment to a purer Christianity, free of the church-state entanglements that have troubled civilization from the Middle Ages through to our own time.

The legacy of Arnold provided a rallying cry 700 years later for those seeking to establish the nation of Italy in the 1860s. In the 1880s, the city of Zurich, where Arnold had preached and taught, contributed to the grand statue of him in Piazzalle Arnaldo, Brescia, to honor Arnold, champion of free thought and apostle of liberty.

Appendix I

Texts of Primary Sources

A. John of Salisbury. *The Historia Pontificalis (Memoirs of the Papal Court)*. Edited and translated with an introduction by Marjorie Chibnall. New York: Thomas Nelson and Sons, 1956.

This document by John of Salisbury covers the activities of the papal court of Eugenius III during the years 1148–1152. The occasion for John of Salisbury's account of Arnold of Brescia is the negotiation between the pope and the people of Rome in 1149.

"Negotiations for peace were proceeding between the pope and the Romans, and numerous legations sped to and fro between the two parties. But there were many obstacles in the way of peace, the greatest of all being the refusal of the Romans to expel Arnold of Brescia who was said to have bound himself by oath to uphold the honour of the city and Roman republic. The Romans in their turn promised him aid and counsel against all men, and explicitly against the lord pope; for the Roman church had excommunicated him and ordered him to be shunned as a heretic. This man was a priest by office, a canon regular by profession, and one who had mortified his flesh with fasting and coarse raiment: of keen intelligence, persevering in his study of the scriptures, eloquent in speech, and a vehement preacher against the vanities of the world.

Appendix I

"Nevertheless he was reputed to be factious and a leader of schism, who wherever he lived prevented the citizens from being at peace with the clergy. He had been abbot of Brescia, and when the bishop was absent on a short visit to Rome had so swayed the minds of the citizens that they would scarcely open their gates to the bishop on his return.

"For this he was deposed by Pope Innocent and expelled from Italy; crossing the Alps into France he became a disciple of Peter Abelard, and together with Master Hyacinth, who is now a cardinal, zealously fostered his cause against the abbot of Clairvaux.

"After Master Peter had set out for Cluny [on his way to appeal to the pope after the Council of Sens], [Arnold] remained at Paris on the Mont-Sainte-Genevieve, expounding the scriptures to scholars at the church of St. Hilary where Peter had been lodged. But he had no listeners except poor students who publicly begged their bread from door to door to support themselves and their master.

"He said things that were entirely consistent with the law accepted by Christian people, but not at all with the life they led. To the bishops he was merciless on account of their avarice and filthy lucre; most of all because of stains on their personal lives, and their striving to build the church of God in blood. He denounced the abbot, [Bernard of Clairvaux] whose name is renowned above all others for his many virtues, as a seeker after vainglory, envious of all who won distinction in learning or religion unless they were his own disciples.

"In consequence the abbot prevailed on the most Christian king to expel him from the Frankish kingdom; from there he returned to Italy after Pope Innocent's death and, after promising reparation and obedience to the Roman church, was received at Viterbo by Pope Eugenius. Penance was imposed on him, which he claimed to have performed in fasts, vigils and prayers in the holy places of the city; and again he took a solemn oath to show obedience.

"Whilst dwelling in Rome under pretext of penance he won the city to his side, and preaching all the more freely because the lord pope was occupied in Gaul he built up a faction known as the heretical sect of the Lombards. He had disciples who imitated his austerities and won favour with the populace through outward decency and austerity of life, but found their chief supporters amongst pious women. He himself was frequently heard on the Capitol and in public gatherings.

"He had already publicly denounced the cardinals, saying that their college, by its pride, avarice, hypocrisy and manifold shame was not the church of God, but a place of business and den of thieves, which took the place of the scribes and Pharisees amongst Christian peoples. The pope himself was not what he professed to be—an apostolic man and shepherd of souls—but a man of blood who maintained his authority by fire and sword, a tormentor of churches and oppressor of the innocent, who did nothing in the world save gratify his lust and empty other men's coffers to fill his own. He was, he said, so far from apostolic that he imitated neither the life nor the doctrine of the apostles, wherefore neither obedience nor reverence was due to him: and in any case no man could be admitted who wished to impose a yoke of servitude on Rome, the seat of Empire, fountain of liberty and mistress of the world" (62–65).

B. Otto of Freising. *The Deeds of Frederick Barbarossa (Gesta Friderici I Imperatoris)*. Translated and annotated with an introduction by Charles Christopher Mierow. New York; Columbia University Press, 1953.

Otto's book covers the reign of Frederick until the author's death in 1158. He mentions Arnold of Brescia twice. The first instance, xxviii (xxvii), page 61, is in reference to a letter from the Roman Senate to Conrad, Frederick Barbarossa's predecessor as King of the Germans, inviting him to Rome to be crowned emperor by their authority. The comment about Arnold precedes the text of the letter, xxix (xxviii), recorded on pages 61 to 63.

First Book, xxviii. "During these days, a certain Arnold, who wore a religious garb but was by no means faithful to it, as was evident from his teaching, entered the city of Rome. Because of his hatred for the honors paid to the Church, and seeking to restore the dignity of the senate and the equestrian order to their ancient status, he aroused almost the entire City, and especially the populace, against his pope. Whence, in corroboration of their rashness, or rather of their folly, there is extant the following document sent by them to their prince" (61).

The second entry concerns the meeting between Pope Adrian [also Hadrian] IV and Frederick Barbarossa at Viterbo in 1155. Frederick had come to Italy and was bound for Rome to be crowned Holy Roman Emperor by

Appendix I

Adrian IV. The focus of Otto's interest in Arnold, therefore, is his presence and activities in Rome at that time, a few years later than the occasion for John of Salisbury's comments above.

Second Book, xxviii. "Now on his way to the City the king encamped near Viterbo. Thither came the Roman pope, Hadrian, with his cardinals, and was received with the honor due to his office. He was given a deferential hearing as he uttered bitter complaints against his people. For the aforesaid people, since their endeavor to reinstate the order of senators, in their rash daring did not shrink from inflicting many outrages on their popes. There was this additional aggravation of their seditious conduct, that a certain Arnold of Brescia, of whom mention has been made above, under guise of religion and—to use the words of the Gospel—acting as wolf in sheep's clothing, entered the City, inflamed to violence the minds of the simple people by his exceedingly seductive doctrines, and induced—nay, rather, seduced—a countless throng to espouse that cause.

"That Arnold, a native of Italy from the city of Brescia, a cleric ordained only as a lector of the church there, had once had Peter Abelard as his teacher. He was a man not indeed dull of intellect, yet abounding rather in profusion of words than in the weight of his ideas; a lover of originality and eager for novelty. The minds of such men are inclined to devise heresies and the tumult of schisms.

"Returning from his studies in France to Italy, he assumed the religious habit that he might deceive the more, assailing all things, carping at everything, sparing no one—a disparager of the clergy and of bishops, a persecutor of monks, a flatterer only of the laity. For he used to say that neither clerics that owned property, nor bishops that had regalia, nor monks with possessions could in any wise be saved. All these things belong to the prince, and should be bestowed of his beneficence for the use of the laity only.

"Besides this, he is said to have held unreasonable views with regard to the sacrament of the altar and infant baptism. While he was keeping the church of Brescia in uproar in these and other ways, which it would take too long to enumerate, and was maliciously defaming ecclesiastical personalities to the laity of that land, who have itching ears as regards the clergy, he was accused by the bishop and pious men of that city at the great council [The Lateran Council of 1139] held at Rome under Innocent. Therefore the Roman pontiff decided that silence should be imposed upon the man, that his pernicious teaching might not spread to more people. And thus it was done.

"So that man, fleeing from Italy, betook himself to the lands beyond the Alps, and there assuming the role of teacher in Zurich, a town of Swabia, he sowed his pernicious doctrine for some time. But when he learned of the death of Innocent he entered the City, near the beginning of the pontificate of Eugenius.

"As he found it aroused to rebellion against its pope, he incited it all the more to revolt, not following the counsel of the wise man who says of a situation of this kind: 'Heap not wood upon his fire' [Ecclesiasticus 8:3].

"He set forth the examples of the ancient Romans, who by virtue of the ripened judgment of the senate and the disciplined integrity of the valiant spirit of youth made the whole world their own. Wherefore he advocated that the Capitol should be rebuilt, the senatorial dignity restored, and the equestrian order reinstituted. Nothing in the administration of the City was the concern of the Roman pontiff; the ecclesiastical courts should be enough for him.

"Moreover, the menace of this baneful doctrine began to grow so strong that not only were the houses and splendid palaces of Roman nobles and cardinals being destroyed, but even the reverend persons of some of the cardinals were shamefully treated by the infuriated populace, and several were wounded. Although he incessantly and irreverently perpetrated these things and others like them for many days (that is, from the death of Celestine until this time) and despised the judgment of the pastors, justly and canonically pronounced against him, as though in his opinion they were void of all authority, at last he fell into the hands of certain men and was taken captive within the limits of Tuscany.

"He was held for trial by the prince and finally was brought to the pyre by the prefect of the City. After his corpse had been reduced to ashes in the fire, it was scattered on the Tiber, lest his body be held in veneration by the mad populace.

"But that my pen may come back to the topic whence it has digressed, after the supreme rulers of the world had been united amid their retinue, they advanced together for several days and pleasant converse was exchanged as between a spiritual father and his son. Both ecclesiastical and secular matters were discussed, as though a single state had been created from two princely courts" (142-144).

An account of the meeting between Frederick and ambassadors of the city and Senate of Rome at Sutri in 1155 follows (144-149).

Appendix I

C. Bernard of Clairvaux. *The Letters of St. Bernard of Clairvaux.* Translated by Bruno Scott James. Chicago: Henry Regnery Company, 1953.

Bernard first mentions Arnold in a letter to Pope Innocent II written after the Council of Sens (1141). Abelard refused to enter into debate at Sens because he knew that Bernard had arranged his condemnation the previous night. Instead, Peter appealed to Rome. Bernard wrote this letter anticipating the visit of Peter and Arnold to the pope. After receiving letters, one from Bernard and another from the bishops, written by Bernard, the pope ordered Arnold and Peter to be confined in separate monasteries. Bernard's personal letter is three-and-a-half-pages long. Portions of it are presented here.

Letter 239

>To Pope Innocent

"To his most loving father and lord, Innocent, by the grace of God Supreme Pontiff, the entire devotion, for what it is worth, of Brother Bernard, styled Abbot of Clairvaux."

1. "There must be scandals; they are an unpleasant necessity. Therefore the Prophet says, 'Had I but wings as the dove has wings, to fly away and be at rest', and the Apostle desires to be dissolved and be with Christ, and Elias declares, 'I can bear no more, Lord; put an end to my life; I have no better right to live than my fathers.' This I have in common with the saints, although it is a matter only of the will and not of merit, that I too wish to be taken out of it all, overcome, I admit, by 'the fears that daunt me and the storm around me.' But I fear that I should not be found so well prepared as I am well disposed. I am weary of life; and I know not whether it would be well for me to die . . .

2. "Fool that I am, I was but now promising myself rest, when the madness of the lion had been quelled and peace restored to the Church. [A reference to Peter Leonis, the former anti-Pope.] And now the Church is at peace, but not I. . . . Grief transcends and never ends for me, my sorrows have increased because evils have gained strength; first the frost, then came the snow. Who can endure this cold? In it charity grows cold so that iniquity abounds.

"We have escaped the lion only to fall victims to the dragon who is, perhaps, more dangerous lurking in his lair than the lion raging in the open. Although he [Abelard] is no longer lurking in his lair: would that his poisonous writings were still lurking in their shelves, and not being discussed at the crossroads! His books have wings: and they who hate the light because their lives are evil, have dashed into the light thinking it was darkness. Darkness is being brought into towns and castles in the place of light; and for honey or poison or, I should say, poison in honey is being offered on all sides to everyone. His writings 'have passed from country to country, and from one kingdom to another.' A new gospel is being forged for foundation is being laid besides that which has been laid. Virtues and vices are being discussed immorally, the sacraments of the Church falsely, the mystery of the Holy Trinity neither simply nor soberly. Everything is put perversely, everything quite differently, and beyond what we have been accustomed to hear.

3. "Goliath advances tall of body, girt in the noble accoutrements of war, and preceded by his armour-bearer, Arnold of Brescia. [James makes the note: "A pupil of Abelard, heretic, and demagogue."] Scale is joined to scale, and there is no breathing space between. The bee that is in France has murmured to the bee in Italy, and they have joined forces against the Lord and against his anointed, 'they have strung their bows, have arrows ready in the quiver, to shoot from their hiding places at unoffending hearts.'

"In food and clothing they have all the appearances of piety, but they reject its virtue, and they deceive all the more people by transforming themselves into angels of light, whereas they are Satan. Therefore Goliath, standing between the two armies with his armour-bearer, cries out with a loud voice to the ranks of Israel, and taunts the forces of the saints, all the more audaciously for there being no David to defy him. He insults the Doctors of the Church by holding up the philosophers for exaggerated praises. He prefers their ideas and his own novelties to the doctrines and faith of the Catholic Fathers; and, when all have fled before him, he calls me out, the least of all, to single combat" (317, 318).

Likely in 1142, Bernard, having forced Arnold out of France by appealing to the king, learned that Arnold was teaching in Zurich. He then wrote the following letter to the Bishop of Constance.

Appendix I

Letter 250

To the Bishop of Constance, Concerning Arnold of Brescia

1. "'If the good man of the house knew at what hour the thief would come, he would surely watch and not suffer his house to be broken into.' Do you know that a thief has broken into your house during the night, not indeed your house but the Lord's house, yet entrusted to you? Surely you do know what is happening amongst you, for the news of it has reached even me who lives such a great distance from you. It is not to be wondered at that you were not able to foresee the hour or observe the nocturnal entry of the thief; but it will be surprising if you do not recognize him when he has been caught, if you do not hold him fast, if you do not stop him from carrying off your vessels, even Christ's most precious possessions: the souls which he has marked with his image and redeemed with his blood.

"Perhaps you are still perplexed and wondering to whom I can be referring. I speak of Arnold of Brescia, a man whom I could wish was as praise-worthy for his doctrine as for his way of life. If you want to know, he is a man who comes neither eating nor drinking, that he may sup alone with the devil of the blood of souls. He is one of those whom the vigilant Apostle noted as having the appearances of virtue but denying the power thereof. And the Lord himself also noted the same thing when he said: 'They come in sheep's clothing, but inwardly they are ravening wolves.'

"Up to the present wherever he has lived for any time he has left behind him such foul and fell tracks, that he dare not on any account return to where he has once set foot. He has quite atrociously stirred up and troubled the land in which he was born. When accused before the lord Pope of a most wicked schism, he was expelled from his birthplace and forced to swear he would not return except by the pope's permission. For a like reason this notable schismatic was turned out of the kingdom of France. Cast off by the Apostle Peter he promptly joined up with Peter Abelard, and with him and before him tried hard and stubbornly to defend his errors which had already been exposed and condemned by the Church.

2. "His madness has not yet abated, his hand is yet stretched out. For, although a fugitive and wanderer, he does not cease to do amongst strangers what he is no longer able to do amongst his own countrymen; like a raging lion he goes about seeking whom he may devour. And now, I am told, he is working iniquity amongst you, and devouring your people like bread. His mouth is full of cursing and bitterness, and his feet are swift to

shed blood; destruction and sorrow are in his ways, and the way of peace he does not know. He is an enemy of Christ's cross, a sower of discord, a fabricator of schism, a disturber of the peace, and a divider of unity. His words are smooth as oil, but they are very weapons of destruction. It is his habit to attract the rich and powerful by soft words and the pretence of virtue, according to those words:

"'He will agree with the rich to lie in wait at dark corners, and kill the man who never wronged him'. When he has obtained their good will and feels sure of their friendship, then you will see the man openly confront the clergy and, with the support of military power, rise up against the bishops themselves, and rage on all side against the ecclesiastical order.

"Knowing this, I do not see what better or more wholesome thing you can do than to follow the advice of the Apostle and 'put away the evil one from amongst you', though the friend of the Bridegroom will see that he is imprisoned rather than put to flight, so that he should not be able to run around doing any more harm. This is the command which our lord the Pope put into writing when he was with us, because of all the evil he had heard of him; but there was no one to do the good work. If we are warned by the Scriptures to catch the little foxes which spoil the vine, how much more is a great and fierce wolf to be bound fast so that he shall not break into the fold and slay and destroy the sheep" (329-331).

The bishop complied and asked Arnold to leave. From Zurich Arnold journeyed to Passau where he was received by Cardinal Guy (Guido), who had been sent as a papal legate to that territory by Innocent II. When Bernard learned of Arnold's presence in Passau, he wrote Guido the following letter sometime between August of 1142, when the Cardinal arrived in Passau, and September of 1143, when Innocent died.

Letter 251

To Cardinal Guy, Legate in Bohemia

"It is reported that Arnold of Brescia is with you, the man whose life is as sweet as honey and whose doctrine is as bitter as poison, the man with the head of a dove and the tail of a scorpion, the man whom Brescia has ejected, Rome rejected, and France repulsed; whom Germany abhors, and Italy will not receive. Have a care, I implore you, that he does not extend his mischievous influence under the cover of your authority. He has both the skill and the will to do it, and if your favour is added we shall have a triple cord such as is not easily broken; and the harm done will be, I fear, beyond measure.

"There are only two alternatives for me, if it is true that you have this man with you: either I must believe that he is not at all known to you, or (what is more likely) that you have hopes of converting him. It is much to be desired that you may succeed in this. But who can fashion a son of Abraham from this stone? What a welcome boon it would be for the Church to receive from your hands as a vessel of honour, one whom she has endured for so long as a vessel of dishonour. You can try; but a prudent man will be careful not to exceed the limit laid down by the Apostle when he says: 'A man that is a heretic, after the first and second admonition, avoid; knowing that he, that is such an one, is subverted, and sinneth, being condemned by his own judgement'.

"Otherwise to be friendly with him, to hold him often in conversation, not to say to entertain him, looks like favouring him, and is a powerful protection for any enemy. A friend of the Apostolic legate and member of his household will put forward with impunity what he likes, and will be readily believed whatever he says. Who would expect any wrong to come from the legate of the lord Pope? And who would dare to oppose one who comes from you, even were he openly to say what is perverse?

2. "Consider too what foul traces this man has left behind him wherever he has been. It was not without reason that the strong hand of the Apostolic See obliged him, a man born in Italy, to cross the Alps, and not to return home. Who is there amongst those with whom he is driven to take refuge who does not heartily wish him back again in his own country? That he should make himself so odious to everyone is a clear justification of the penalty under which he lies, so that no one can say that this was inveigled from the Pope.

What possible excuse can there be for flouting the judgement of the Supreme Pontiff? The actions, if not the tongue, of him against whom it was proclaimed testifies to its rightness. And so, to favour this man is to contradict the Pope and even the Lord God. A just sentence justly delivered by anyone soever, certainly proceeds from him who says in the words of the Prophet: 'I am one who speaks justice'. I have every confidence in your prudence and uprightness and do not doubt that, when you have learned the truth of the matter from this letter, you will be firm and act in a way that is becoming to yourself and beneficial to the Church of God, on whose behalf you are discharging the office of legate. You command my affection and may count upon my service" (331, 332).

D. The Bergamese Poet. "*Gesta di federico primi in Italia.*" Translated by Mary Martin McLaughlin. In Ross, James, Bruce and Mary Martin McLaughlin, Editors. *The Portable Medieval Reader,* **341–344. New York: Viking, 1960.**

This Latin poem celebrating Frederick's adventures in Italy, came to light and was published by E. Monaci in 1887. The occasion for this section of the poem about Arnold was his execution in 1155. No attempt has been made to recreate the poetry.

"This man [Arnold of Brescia] was harshly austere throughout his whole life; moderate in his habits, yet in his speech extravagant, he strove for wisdom beyond that which is fitting. He was eloquent and bold and self-assured, a man of much reading. I believe that it is just to describe briefly his teaching and his end, for it will please many to know it.

"He attacked and condemned priests as well as lesser people. Believing that he alone lived righteously and that others erred unless they wished to follow his teaching, he also attacked violently the actions of the prelates, and, in short, he spared no one, he mingled the true with the false, and was pleasing to many.

"He condemned the laymen for not paying their tithes, and he condemned all taking of usury. Following the Scripture, he taught that shameful greed, war, hatred, lust, perjury, murder, theft, deception, and the evil desires of the flesh are hindrances to eternal life. He spared no vice, and like a foolish doctor, he cut away the healthy along with the diseased. For he censured all priests as wicked and as followers of that Simon who wanted to buy divine things for money, and he made almost no exceptions . . . He said that the monks were completely irregular, and that truly they could not be called by the name of monks.

"He declared that the great prelates coveted transitory things, and scorned the things of heaven for those of earth; night and day, they judged legal cases for a price, and considered the office of the episcopate of less account than this. For this, he claimed, they would be condemned to

Appendix I

everlasting death, and he asserted that all men of every order were corrupted, loving neither God nor their neighbours.

"He cried out that, alas, evils flourished especially in the Roman see, where money was honoured more than justice, and where money was obtained in place of justice. There evil had spread from the head to the body, and all the members sought money and bribes. All things were done with money, the things of the Lord were bought and sold, and anyone who lacked money was completely despised.

"This was the teaching of that famous Master Arnold, which pleased many men only because of its novelty. Indeed, Europe was now full of this doctrine. He first gathered bitter fruits in his native city, and you, Brescia have reveled in the teaching of your citizen. He also stirred up great Milan, and the Roman people, always willing to believe new things. Wherever he was, this man caused sedition, for he deceived people under the image of truth.

"The highest apostolic shepherd wished to convert him, yet he could not. And with kind words he frequently admonished him to give up his error and his evil doctrine. But Arnold never ceased to insult the holy father with bitter words, and he did not abandon his wicked teaching. And when, often warned, he became worse, and rejoiced that his fame spread through the world, the pope, grieving because the people were corrupted by false teaching, and wishing to cure the sickness by reason, expelled this schismatic teacher from the bosom of his mother, the Church. Desirous that the rest of the body should retain its health, the wise doctor cut off with a sword the diseased member.

"But the tongue of Master Arnold was not so restrained that he did not spread his customary errors, that he did not snap harder with bared fangs at the Roman Church, that he did not teach the people in opposition to the lord pope. Then he was brought by King Frederick [Barbarossa] to the Roman judge who had been appointed, and was put in chains. And the ruler ordered his case to be judged, and the learned teacher was condemned for his teaching.

"But when he saw that his punishment was prepared, and that his neck was to be bound in the halter by hurrying fate, and when he was asked if he would renounce his false doctrine, and confess his sins after the manner of the wise, fearless and self-confident, wonderful to relate, he replied that his own doctrine seemed to him sound, nor would he hesitate to undergo death for his teachings, in which there was nothing absurd or dangerous.

"And he requested a short delay for time to pray, for he said that he wished to confess his sins to Christ. Then on bended knees, with eyes and hands raised up to heaven, he groaned, sighing from the depths of his breast, and silently communed in spirit with God, commending to Him his soul. And after a short time, prepared to suffer with constancy, he surrendered his body to death. Those who looked on at his punishment shed tears; even the executioners were moved by pity for a little time, while he hung from the noose which held him. And it is said that the king, moved too late by compassion, mourned over this.

"Learned Arnold, what did such great learning profit you, and so much fasting, and so many labours? Of what profit was such a hard life, which spurned all slothful leisure and enjoyed no fleshly pleasures? Alas, what made you turn your biting slander upon the Church, so that you should come, O wretched one, to the sad noose! Behold your doctrine, O condemned one, for which you have paid the penalty! Doctrine passes away, and your teaching will not long survive! It has been burned and dissolved with you into a few ashes, lest perchance something might be left to be honoured."

E. Walter Map. *De Nugis Curialium, (Courtiers' Trifles)*. Translated by Frederick Tupper and Marbury Bladen Oghle. London: Chatto & Windus, 1924.

In *Courtiers' Trifles* Walter Map gives an account of the discourse at a dinner hosted by Thomas Becket, Archbishop of Canterbury. At this dinner, one of two Cistercians abbots in attendance read the letter from Bernard of Clairvaux to Pope Innocent concerning Peter Abelard and his armour bearer, Arnold (see I. C. above). The Cistercians praised Bernard to the distress of another guest, John Planeta, and, presumably, Walter Map, who, after relating the unflattering stories told by Planeta about Bernard, tells his readers about Arnold. This dinner occurred, in all likelihood, sometime between 1162 and 1164. The focus of the story is Arnold's activity in Rome after 1146.

"Since the name of Arnold of Brescia was mentioned above in our discourse, let us tell, if you please, who he was, just as we heard the story from a man of his time—a great man too, and one of high learning, Robert of Burneham. This Arnold was summoned after Abelard by Pope Eugenius, was allowed no defence, and, in his absence, was condemned, not for his writings, but for his preaching. In the matter of birth this Arnold was high-born and noble, in the matter of learning he was without a peer, in the matter of piety he was chief, permitting himself no indulgence in food or raiment, save when the strictest necessity compelled.

"He went about preaching, 'seeking not the things which are his but those which are God's,' and he came to be loved and respected by all. When he went to Rome, the Romans heard his teaching with reverence. He finally came to the papal court and saw the tables of the cardinals loaded with vessels of silver and gold, and the dainties at their feasts; in the presence of their lord the Pope he chided them kindly, but they bore it unkindly and cast him out; he returned to the city and began to teach without flagging.

"The people of the city assembled to hear him and 'heard him gladly.' It came to pass that the people heard that Arnold had preached a sermon on the contempt of rewards and riches into the ears of the cardinals in the presence of their lord the Pope, and had been cast out by the cardinals, so they gathered before the court (Curia) and cried out against the Pope and the cardinals, saying that Arnold was a good man and just, they greedy, unjust, and wicked, men who were not 'the light of the world' but the lees, and much else after the same manner, and scarcely did they withhold their hands.

"After this outbreak had been with difficulty quieted, ambassadors were sent to the Emperor, with the Pope's denunciation of Arnold as excommunicate and a heretic, and these messengers did not withdraw until they had him hanged" (49, 50).

F. Wezel (Wetzel). Letter to King Frederick. Philipp Jaffe, ed. *Bibliotheca Rerum Germanicarum*, Vol. I, *Monumenta Corbeiensia, Wibaldi Epistolae*, 404:539–543, translated by Mary Preuss.

This letter was written after Frederick Barbarossa succeeded Conrad III in 1152. The author was a colleague of Arnold (some have speculated that Arnold himself was the author). Most scholars agree that this letter represents Arnold's teaching.

"To the most Exalted, by the Grace of God, Frederick, Wezel, may you gain every advantage in soul and body."

Texts of Primary Sources

"I am very happy that your nation has elevated you to its kingship. As to the rest, I grieve that at advice of the clerics and monks whose divine and human ideas are mixed up, you have not consulted as you ought, the most holy city, ruler and mistress of the world, creator and mother of all rulers, about this matter. And that you have not requested her confirmation and approval, her through whom all rulers rule and without whom no rulers rule. Nor, have you written to her as a son ought to write to his mother, if indeed you have proposed yourself to be her son and minister.

"For who is able to obtain a stable order except the person Rebecca has chosen and promoted. Granted that father Isaac wished and strove to prefer Esau by his blessing, Jacob, at the call of his mother, and with himself fearful that the advice regarding it was foolish or useless, obtained the blessing and the lordship, since Esau had made a delay in hunting and he was left with regrets. In order that I may come quickly to the point, I will set out to you more fully what I am saying if you will listen carefully.

"Your calling, that is to be a ruler and that of all your predecessors, I say, is from blind heretics, that is the Julianists and apostate clerics, and it is done by false monks lying and betraying their order by taking authority against the gospel and canonical laws and claiming power by laws, as much human as divine, disturbing the church of God and secular matters.

"Moreover, that that is how things are, blessed Peter shows. Peter whose representatives they falsely claim to be. 'That through these you may escape from the corruption that is in the world because of passion . . . supplement your faith with virtue, and virtue with knowledge, and knowledge with self-control, and self-control with steadfastness, and steadfastness with godliness, and godliness with brotherly affection, and brotherly affection with love' (II Peter 1:4-7).

"Let these things rule you, for the person to which these things are not to hand is blind and groping in the dark. Concerning which things the apostle says: 'There will be false teachers (2:1), and in their greed they will exploit you with false words (2:13) reveling in their dissipation, carousing with you (2:14). They have eyes full of adultery (2:2), and because of them the way of truth will be reviled (2:17), these are waterless springs and mists driven by a storm (2:17).' How are such people able to say with Peter 'Behold we have left all and followed you' (Matt. 19:27) and 'Silver and gold have I none' (Acts 3:6)? How can they hear from the Lord 'You are the light of the world, you are the salt of the earth' (Matt 5:13, 14)? To whom what follows applies too much: 'But if the salt has lost its taste, how shall its saltness be restored? It is no longer good for anything except to be thrown out and trodden under foot by men.'—and by pigs.

"Hence John says, 'He who says he abides in him ought to walk in the same way in which he walked' (I John 2:6). Likewise, 'He who says, "I know him" and does not keep his commandments is a liar and the truth is not in him' (2:4). It is said by the Lord to Peter and to the representatives of Peter, 'As the father has sent me, so send I you' (John 20:21). But in like manner he himself that was sent by the father said, 'If I am not doing the works of my father, then do not believe me' (John 10:37). If one should not believe Christ, who did no sin, unless there are works, how can one believe those who not only do things badly, but even do bad things publicly? Hence it is said, 'How are you able to speak good things when you are evil?' Just as the Lord himself said: 'How are you able to believe when you are each seeking your own glory' (John 5:44)? 'For faith itself without works is dead' (James 2:17).

"How in the world can those who not only covet or enviously desire all riches but who have also destroyed the riches which existed safely through whose use there was such great and widespread peace throughout the whole world that it placed the Son of God from the bosom of his father into the bosom of his mother, who have destroyed this wealth by their false teaching, by living in a luxurious, degenerate way, how are they able to hear or to listen to that first of all the gospel's commands, 'Blessed are the poor in Spirit' when they themselves are not poor by any stretch of the imagination? Hence blessed Jerome says, 'Flee the clerical business man, either one who has become rich out of poverty or one who has become famous out of obscurity, flee him like the plague.'

"How can those who are pressing their energies toward secular business be able to fulfill the first decree of all the Roman Popes which is set out by blessed Clement in his first epistle or that is promulgated by blessed Peter the Apostle? How can they possibly fulfill that, deaf hearers that they are? Among the other things, which indeed Peter commanded Clement, he enjoined the following, saying: 'You ought, indeed, yourself to live blamelessly and to strive with highest zeal to cast away from yourself all the business of this life. You should not stand bail for anyone, you should not be an advocate in a law suit nor in any other occupation of worldly business.

"'For Christ does not command you today to be a judge nor a person who is well acquainted with secular business lest, focusing your attention on human cares of the present time, you are not able to leave yourself open to the Word of God or to find time for it.

"'These things which we have said should pertain less to you. Let the laity take over these responsibilities and let no one make you busy drawing you from these studies to undertake secular cares, even those which pertain to the employment of common life. Make yourself free without care in all of these things in which you ought not to be involved. Let everybody work on them together. But if by chance the laity do not understand these things, they ought to be taught by the deacons and to you should be the cares of the church. For if you get occupied with worldly cares, you deceive both yourself and those who hear you. For you are not able to distinguish sufficiently those things which pertain to salvation and the result will be both that you will be put down from office and that your students will perish through ignorance. Therefore, leave yourself free for this alone that you teach the word of God without ceasing.'

"In truth that lie and heretical tale in which it is related that Constantine yielded imperial authority to Silvester by simony was so well known in the city that even mercenaries and poor women argued with people as learned as you please about it. And the apostolic word on this subject with its cardinals did not dare to appear in the city for shame. Indeed, the holy Meliciades, the predecessor of the holy Silvester, in his writings asserts that Constantine was baptized, saying: 'When among the confusion of the world, the church began to increase, it came to such a level that the Roman rulers hastened to the faith of Christ and the sacrament of baptism among whom that most religious man, Constantine was the first to adopt the true faith.' Indeed, the Tripartite history testifies that he became a Christian before he himself entered the city as its emperor.

"Listen to what I say. Esau, not spending his free time at home and ignoring the teaching and advice of his mother seeking forest places and called by a blind man, lacks the promises (blessing) up until now. Jacob in turn, obedient to his mother, covering neck and hands with the household covering of teaching, snatches away surreptitiously those things which the blind man had promised to the man of the forest. He snatches them away with divine assent.

"Julian [Justinian], the emperor, bears witness that the emperor ought not to be a forest man but somebody who is experienced in law. Julian, the emperor, in the first line of all his laws says: 'The authority of imperial rule ought to be adorned and armed not only by weapons, but also by laws. So that in either a time of war or a time of peace, it is governed properly (rightly).'

Appendix I

"A little later, he shows, likewise, that the Roman ruler has the rule and the right to make laws. But also, that he should have the strength of the law and implies it is because the people have yielded to him all their power and authority. But since the authority and dignity of the whole state are of the Romans and since the title of emperor is something from the Romans—not that the Romans belong to the emperor, but the emperor is derived from the Romans—what follows seems to be left out of the thinking about it. What law or reason prevents the senate and people from creating an emperor?

"Do not hesitate to send to Rome as quickly as you can comrade Rudulf of Ravensburg and comrade Ulrich of Lenzburg and other suitable people, perhaps Eberhard of Bodmen, those who have knowledge of the law of the empire and who dare to treat about it. Lest something new (a rebellion) arise against you there, take care to prevent it."

G. Otto of Freising. *The Deeds of Frederick Barbarossa*.

The Speech of the Roman Envoys to King Frederick

"'We the ambassadors of the City—no insignificant part of the City—O Excellent King, have been sent to Your Excellency by the senate and people of Rome. Hear with calm mind and gracious ears what is brought to your attention by the City that is the kindly mistress of the world—the City of which, by God's aid, you shall soon be prince, emperor, and lord. If you have come—nay, because, as I [the People] believe, you have come—in peace, I rejoice.

"'You seek authority over the world; I arise willingly to give you the crown. I meet you with rejoicing. For why should not a prince come peacefully to visit his people? Why should he not treat with notable munificence the people who have awaited his coming with great and protracted expectation, in order to shake off the unseemly yoke of the clergy? I pray for the return of former times. I ask for the return of the privileges of the renowned City. May the City under this prince take the helm of the world once more. May the insolence of the world be checked under this emperor and be subjected to the sole rule of the City! May such a ruler be adorned with the fame as well as with the name of Augustus!

"'Now you know that the city of Rome, by the wisdom of the senatorial dignity and the valor of the equestrian order, sending out her boughs from sea to sea, has not only extended her empire to the ends of the earth but has even added to her world the islands that lie beyond the world, and planted there the shoots of her dominion. The boisterous waves of the seas could not protect those, nor could the rugged and inaccessible crags of the Alps defend these: indomitable Roman valor has subdued all.

"But, for our sins, since our princes dwelt at a great distance from us [Constantinople], that noble token of our antiquity—I refer to the senate—was given over to neglect by the slothful carelessness of certain men. As wisdom slumbered, strength too was of necessity diminished. I have arisen to reinstate the holy senate of the holy City and the equestrian order, to enhance your glory and that of the divine republic, that by the decree of the one and the arms of the other its ancient splendor may return to the Roman empire and to your person. Should this not please Your Nobility? Will not so notable a deed and one so in keeping with your authority be judged even worthy of reward?

"'Hear then, O Prince, with patience and with clemency a few matters that have to do with your justice and with mine! About yours, however, before I speak of mine. For "the beginning is from Jove." You were a stranger. I made you a citizen. You were a newcomer from the regions beyond the Alps. I have established you as prince. What was rightfully mine I gave to you. You ought therefore first afford security for the maintenance of my good customs and ancient laws, strengthened for me by the emperors your predecessors, that they may not be violated by the fury of barbarians. To my officials, who must acclaim you on the Capitol, you should give as much as five thousand pounds as expense money. You should avert harm from the republic even to the extent of the shedding of your blood, and safeguard all this by privileges, and establish it by the interposition of an oath with your own hand'" (145, 146).

Frederick's reply to the Roman Delegation

"Hereupon, the king, inflamed with righteous anger by the tenor of a speech as insolent as it was unusual, interrupted the flow of words of those ambassadors concerning the jurisdiction of their republic and of the empire . . . as they [the Romans] were about to spin out their oration in the Italian fashion by lengthy and circuitous periods, . . . replied without preparation but not unprepared.

"'We have heard much heretofore concerning the wisdom and the valor of the Romans, yet more concerning their wisdom. Wherefore we

Appendix I

cannot wonder enough at finding your words insipid with swollen pride rather than seasoned with the salt of wisdom. You set forth the ancient renown of your city. You extol to the very stars the ancient status of your sacred republic. Granted, granted! To use the words of your own writer, "There was, *there was once* virtue in this republic." "Once," I say. And O that we might truthfully and freely say "now!" Your Rome—nay, ours also—has experienced the vicissitudes of time. She could not be the only one to escape a fate ordained by the Author of all things for all that dwell beneath the orb of the moon.'"

[Frederick continued his speech, whose length exceeded the length of the Roman speech responding point by point to the Roman assertions and demands. Asserting that what was in Rome belongs to the Franks.]

"'Not yet has the hand of the Franks or the Germans been made weak.' There is no reason, he continues, for him to take an oath to observe the laws since it is under willingness to protect the laws and the fatherland that he has become king. And, 'that I should personally swear to pay you a certain sum of money. How disgraceful!'"

Otto concluded his report:

"With these words, and not without a justifiable indignation of spirit, he brought his speech to an end and was silent" (146–149).

Appendix II

Arnold's Student Days with Peter Abelard in Paris

EVIDENCE THAT IN HIS youth Arnold was a student of Peter Abelard in is youth comes from a contemporary, Otto of Freising (1110–1158). "Arnold, a native of Italy from the city of Brescia, a cleric ordained only as a lector there, had once had Peter Abelard for a teacher. . . . Returning from his studies in France to Italy, he assumed the religious habit."[1]

Some historians think Otto had it wrong. Absence of collaboration in other primary sources and the fact that Otto is not always reliable, reinforce their skepticism. Historian Giovanni Alfieri, a Brescian native, stated unequivocally that Arnold was *not* a student of Abelard as a youth and that the first meeting of the two occurred after Arnold's exile from Italy in 1139. In *Storia di Brescia*, he wrote: "There doesn't exist any certain evidence of his stay in France prior to his expulsion from Brescia, nor of his contacts with Abelardo. . . . He then went to France where he met, then and *not prior* [emphasis added], Abelardo, or at least Abelardo's ideas, which he defended just as they were being condemned by the council of Sens."[2]

This conclusion is based primarily on the absence of mention of student days by Bernard of Clairvaux and John of Salisbury. One would expect Bernard to use such a fact as further proof of the extent of their association and their conniving against the church.

John of Salisbury, an admirer and former student of Peter Abelard, provided a rather full account of account of Arnold's life, but did not mention that Arnold had been a student of Peter. John knew Arnold personally.

1. Otto, 143.
2. Alfieri, *Storia di Brescia*, 593, 594.

Appendix II

He also knew Arnold had collaborated with Peter prior to and at the Council of Sens. Why didn't he mention student days?

Because of the silence of both these authorities, Alfieri and others have concluded that there were no earlier days and that Otto of Freising did not have his facts straight.

Reginald Lane Poole (1857–1939), eminent historian and author of *Illustrations in Chronology and History*, wrote: "Of Arnold's early life we have no information, except that he was born at Brescia and entered minor orders." But as with student days in Paris, we hear of minor orders only from Otto. Poole continued, "Otto of Freising says that he became a pupil of Abelard in France, a statement which in itself is *not improbable* [emphasis added] but which may be due to a confusion with the later years in which he was certainly associated with the Paris master."[3]

At this point, it may seem that Poole has pretty much dismissed an association of young Arnold with Peter Abelard, but, for the record, he has not. This can be established by observing his use of "*may* be due" and from the more significant fact that he continued to relate Arnold's story based on Otto's account. "Returning to Italy, he became a priest and a canon, and in time abbot, of an Augustinian house at Brescia."[4]

From where would Arnold be "returning to Italy" if student days are dismissed? Otto's account of Arnold's early days needs either to be considered reliable or not. One can't both use it and dismiss it. It seems Poole, in this instance, has not done his usual penetrating analysis *because* he is interested in a *different matter*—as is John of Salisbury—the matter being Arnold's activities in Rome around 1150.

As to Bernard, who was motivated to attack both these men, it has been argued that his omission of an earlier association which could be used to strengthen his case, means the event did not happen. This argument does *not* stand up as evidence.

Abelard had thousands of students over the years. That Bernard would know about Arnold of Brescia studying in Paris in, say, 1115, when he was engaged in founding Clairvaux, is most unlikely. Bernard became aware of Arnold when he came to Paris as colleague of Peter Abelard.

---

3. Poole, "Arnold of Brescia and the Establishment of the Roman Senate", in *H. P.*, Preface, lviii.

4. Ibid., lvii, lix.

John of Salisbury did not mention an earlier connection between Arnold and Peter, if there was one, because it was irrelevant. His purpose was to describe the conflict between the City of Rome and Pope Eugenius.

To deny that Arnold was Peter's student, one has to explain *why Peter took Arnold in as a co-teacher at Mont-Sainte-Geneviève* at a time when Peter was under attack by people such as Bernard. How likely is it that Peter would have accepted Arnold as a colleague without knowing him? Arnold had just been exiled by the pope and had a reputation as a trouble-maker. As we know, Bernard exploited this as a huge strike against Abelard.

And why would Arnold, who had a reputation for purity of life, seek out Abelard, the castrated man who had committed adultery? Without a previous relationship, it is extremely hard to understand the two becoming colleagues in 1139. Surely they already knew each other, and Otto provides written evidence of their previous association.

Greenaway concluded: "To reject [Otto's] very explicit statement in the absence of any other evidence to the contrary merely because no corroboration is available from other sources would scarcely be in accord with the canons of scholarship." He added: "Neither Gregorovius nor Giesebrecht [eminent historians of the period] shows any disposition to impugn the validity of Otto's statement."[5]

---

5. Greenaway, *Arnold*, 30.

Appendix III

Heloise d' Argenteuil and Peter Abelard

It was about 1117 when Heloise d' Argenteuil and Peter Abelard fell in love. She was a young woman in her twenties,[1] in love with learning, and known widely as an accomplished scholar. She lived with her Uncle Fulbert, a canon of Notre Dame. Arrangements were made for Peter to lodge in Fulbert's house and tutor Heloise. In addition to Latin classics and theology, they educated one another in the art of love.

As one would expect, when Uncle Fulbert discovered their affair he evicted Peter. The couple clandestinely continued their relationship, wrote often,[2] and Heloise became pregnant. When she realized her condition, she wrote Peter a letter "full of rejoicing."[3] Afraid of Fulbert, Peter secretly sent Heloise to his sister in Brittany where she gave birth to their son, Astrolabe. Peter promised Fulbert he would marry Heloise. He traveled to Brittany to ask her to marry him and to come back with him to Paris. Heloise opposed marriage because she was certain it would not satisfy her uncle, she thought Peter should continue to devote himself to philosophy, and she did not want to become a wife.

Heloise loved Peter deeply, but she opposed the limitations marriage and family would place on his work as a philosopher. Peter reported her objections in his autobiography. For example::

---

1. Mews, *The Lost Love Letters of Heloise and Abelard*, 32.

2. Mews collected 113 letters that are generally accepted as letters exchanged during the couples' courtship.

3. Abelard, *The Story of My Misfortunes*, Radice Ed., 69.

Then, turning from the consideration of such hindrances to the study of philosophy, Heloise bade me observe what were the conditions of honourable wedlock. What possible concord could there be between scholars and domestics, between authors and cradles, between books or tablets and distaffs, between the stylus or the pen and the spindle? What man, intent on his religious or philosophical meditations, can possibly endure the whining of children, the lullabies of the nurse seeking to quiet them, or the noisy confusion of family life? Who can endure the continual untidiness of children?[4]

Heloise, by Peter's account, marshaled thoughts and experiences of the great philosophers to support her argument. He quoted her as follows: "Seneca, in his advice to Lucilius, says: 'Philosophy is not a thing to be studied only in hours of leisure; we must give up everything else to devote ourselves to it, for no amount of time is really sufficient thereto'" (Epist. 73). Heloise also reminded Peter:

Remember that Socrates was chained to a wife, and by what a filthy accident he himself paid for this blot on philosophy, in order that others thereafter might be made more cautious by his example. Jerome thus mentions this affair, writing about Socrates in his first book against Jovinianus: "Once when he was withstanding a storm of reproaches which Xantippe was hurling at him from an upper story, he was suddenly drenched with foul slops; wiping his head, he said only, "I knew there would be a shower after all that thunder."[5]

Heloise was serious, brilliant, and had a sense of humor. She wanted freedom and independence. She was a scholar, too. She feared marriage would be the end of that for them both. As it turned out, from Peter's point of view, marriage with separation was the answer because it would free them both, as he saw it, for scholarly pursuits.

Peter overrode her arguments and the couple returned from Brittany to Paris, where they married privately. Agreeing to keep the secret, Fulbert attended the wedding. To keep their marriage secret, apparently for Peter's career reasons, the couple did not live together. The unhappy Uncle Fulbert broke the promise of secrecy. Heloise cursed her uncle and swore that her kin were "speaking the most absolute lies. Her uncle, aroused to fury thereby, visited her repeatedly with punishments."[6] When he discovered

4. Abelard, *The Story of My Misfortunes*, Bellows translation, 25.
5. Ibid., 28.
6. Ibid., 29.

Appendix III

this, Peter sent Heloise to the convent at Argenteuil, where she had lived as a young girl. According to Abelard, Fulbert misunderstood; he thought Peter wanted to put Heloise away in a convent to be free of her, so Fulbert arranged his own punishment. He and his friends attacked Abelard one night and, as Peter described it, they "had vengeance on me with a most cruel and most shameful punishment, such as astounded the whole world, for they cut off those parts of my body with which i had done that which was the cause of their sorrow."[7]

Peter subsequently entered the abbey of St. Denys. Although he had difficulty getting along with his fellow monks, he was able to make good use of the monastery's library to write. Not everything he wrote went over well. Pursued by envious old enemies for heretical teaching, he was called before a council at Soisson in 1121, censured, and required to publicly burn his book on the Trinity.

He did not teach for a time until he created a place he called the Paraclete in 1122, on land in the wilderness of Champagne near Troyes, given him by the local bishop. He named it the Paraclete because the Holy Spirit, the Comfortor, had provided comfort to him in his great need.[8] Students soon flocked to the countryside to attend his lectures; they built huts, other buildings, and an oratory (small chapel).

The student body continued to grow, Abelard's success became known, and his enemies came after him again. He escaped by accepting the position of Abbot of St. Gildas de Rhuys in 1127. Without going into detail, it was as if he had jumped from the frying pan into the fire.[9]

Meanwhile, against her wishes, Heloise took vows and became the prioress of a community of nuns at the Abbey of Argenteuil. Abbot Suger of St. Denis acquired Argenteuil in 1129, and dismissed the women. When Peter learned of this, he invited Heloise "along with some other nuns from the same convent who would not leave her, to come to the Paraclete [which was not in use]; and once they had gathered there . . . handed it over to them as a gift."[10] This was the first time in ten years that Peter and Heloise had seen each other.

Heloise and her colleagues made a go of things and the Paraclete gained solid footing. Peter wrote: "Their life there was full of hardship at

---

7. Ibid., 30.
8. Abelard, *The Story of My Misfortunes*, Radice, Ed, 84.
9. Ibid., 94.
10. Ibid., 97.

first and for awhile they suffered the greatest deprivation, but soon God, who they served devoutly, in his mercy brought them comfort; he showed himself a true Paraclete to them too in making the local people sympathetic and kindly disposed towards them. Indeed, I fancy that their worldly goods were multiplied more in a single year than mine would have been in a hundred."[11]

In 1132 Peter wrote *Historia Calamitatis* (*The Story of My Misfortunes*), an autobiographical letter from which comes most of this story. His stated intention was to console a friend by showing his friend that his troubles were slight in comparison with Abelard's calamities. He related his academic career which went from victory to victory until his affair with Heloise, castration, theological attacks upon him, and threats on his life.

Upon receiving a copy of his story, Heloise wrote Peter, "No one, I think, could read or hear it dry-eyed; my own sorrows are renewed by the detail in which you have told it and are redoubled because you say your perils are still increasing."[12] She urged him to write her personally and often, expressed her great sorrow at losing her life with him, and related her state of mind and spirit. Here is a taste of her spirit, the depth of her love, and her eloquence:

> I simply wanted you, nothing of yours. I looked for no marriage-bond, no marriage portion, and it was not my own pleasures and wishes I sought to gratify, as you well know, but yours. The name of wife may seem more sacred or more binding, but sweeter for me will always be the word mistress, or, if you will permit me, that of concubine or whore.[13]
>
> In my case, the pleasures of lovers which we shared have been too sweet—they can never displease me, and can scarcely be banished from my thoughts. Wherever I turn they are always there before my eyes, bringing with them awakened longings and fantasies which will not even let me sleep. Even during the celebration of the Mass, when our prayers should be purer, lewd visions of those pleasures take such a hold upon my unhappy soul that my thoughts are on their wantonness instead of on prayers. I should be groaning over the sins I have committed, but I can only sigh for what I have lost.[14]

11. Ibid.
12. Heloise, Personal Letter 1, Radice, Ed., 110.
13. Heloise, 113
14. Ibid., 133

Appendix III

The Prioress of the Paraclete added, "It was your command, not love of God which made me take the veil."[15]

It is ironic that Peter, the seducer who wrote that his "unbridled lust" prevailed "even when you were unwilling, resisted to the utmost of your power and tried to dissuade me, as yours were the weaker nature I often forced you to consent with threats and blows,"[16] became the one who rejected their times of bliss. Peter intended to put what he called his sin behind him. He was not drawn to recalling the pleasures of loving Heloise. Or, if he was, he did not acknowledge it. He wanted Heloise to agree that things had worked out wonderfully because both of them had found religious vocations. He referred to her as "Heloise—now my sister in Christ rather than my wife."[17] Ignoring her exultation in their past love life, he pursued what he considered to be the course of rectitude and religion and urged her to do the same.

In personal letter 4, he wrote Heloise: "I come at last to what I have called your old perpetual complaint, in which you presume to blame God for the manner of our entry into religion instead of wishing to glorify him as you justly should."[18] He continued, confessing his lust and praising the grace of God for having that part of him removed in order to:

> . . . cut me off from the slough of filth in which I had been wholly immersed in mind as in body. Only thus could I become more fit to approach the holy altars now that no contagion of carnal impurity would ever again call me from them. How mercifully did he want me to suffer so much only in that member, the privation of which would also further the salvation of my soul without defiling my body nor preventing any performance of my duties! Indeed, it would make me readier to perform whatever can be honourably done by setting me wholly free from the heavy yoke of carnal desire.[19]

Thus Peter urged Heloise: "Come too, my inseparable companion, and join me in thanksgiving, you who were made my partner both in guilt and in grace." "See then how greatly the Lord was concerned for us, as if he were reserving us for some great ends, and was indignant or grieved because our

---

15. Ibid., 134
16. Abelard, 147.
17. Abelard, *Misfortunes*, 96.
18. Abelard, 145.
19. Ibid., 148.

knowledge of letters, the talents which he had entrusted to us, were not being used to glorify his name."[20]

With this Heloise reluctantly yielded. She wrote "To him who is especially her lord, she who is uniquely his."

> I would not want to give you cause for finding me disobedient in anything, so I have set the bridle of your injunction on the words which issue from my unbounded grief; thus in writing at least I may moderate what it is difficult or rather impossible to forestall in speech. For nothing is less under our control than the heart—having no power to command it we are forced to obey. . . . I will therefore hold my hand from writing words which I cannot restrain my tongue from speaking; would that a grieving heart would be as ready to obey as a writer's hand![21]

Thus began the set of letters called "Letters of Direction." In this long, erudite letter, Heloise requested guidance in adapting the Rule of Benedict to women in community, explained why it was needed, and asked for resources for their worship. Peter responded with guidance, instruction, hymns, and liturgies for the sisters. His letters of direction are found in the Radice edition, pages 159–269.

But, there is more. Constant Mews, a medieval scholar from New Zealand, has convincingly identified a batch of letters written to each other by Heloise and Abelard *before* their wedding. There are at least two recent books that contain these letters and tell the fascinating story of how they came to light: *The Lost Love Letters of Heloise and Abelard* by Constant J. Mews and *Heloise & Abelard: A New Biography* by James Burge.

Both authors agree these letters were compiled by Johannes de Vepria (ca. 1445–ca. 1518) as part of a collection or handbook of variously purposed letters demonstrating correct form. In this letter-writing manual, "[He] followed a number of staid but worthy examples of good letter-writing with something different: a section that he headed 'From the Letters of Two Lovers.'"[22] The letters are identified by "Man" or "Woman"—no names. There are 113 letters in the letters of lovers section which, according to Mews and Burge, are the letters of passion referred to by Heloise, when in Letter 1 of the personal letters, she chided Peter for his failure to communicate. "When you sought me out for sinful pleasures, your letters came to

20. Ibid., 149
21. Heloise, 159.
22. James Burge, *Heloise and Abelard*, 3.

Appendix III

me thick and fast, and your many songs put your Heloise on everyone's lips, so that every street and house echoed with my name. Is it not far better now to summon me to God than it was then to satisfy our lust?"[23] Note "our." As always, Heloise was ready to own her part—about half of the letters were written by her.

Did Heloise blame God for her fate? She certainly did sometimes. Maybe Peter thought she blamed him. Other than acknowledging his lust along with her own, she does not blame him for their affair, but she is entirely unwilling to speak of her religious vocation as her first or primary desire. It was not. Peter was the reason she was a nun.

Nevertheless, she took it on and became an exemplary, beloved, and respected prioress. Both Peter the Venerable and Bernard of Clairvaux visited her and the sisters at the Paraclete. They praised them, and offered support and advice. Heloise accepted her role as prioress and fulfilled it, but was not willing to say she chose it.

Peter continued teaching and writing until 1141, when he was condemned at Sens. He came into the care of Peter the Venerable, he and Bernard reconciled, and Master Peter died in 1142. His body was taken to the Paraclete for burial. After a distinguished career, Heloise died twenty-two years later (1164) at her post as Abbess of the Paraclete. She was buried along side her husband. Their remains were moved several times over the nine centuries since; they now rest at the cemetery of Père Lachaise, Paris.

---

23. Heloise, 117, 118.

Appendix IV

Maps and Illustrations

A: Map of Paris in 1180

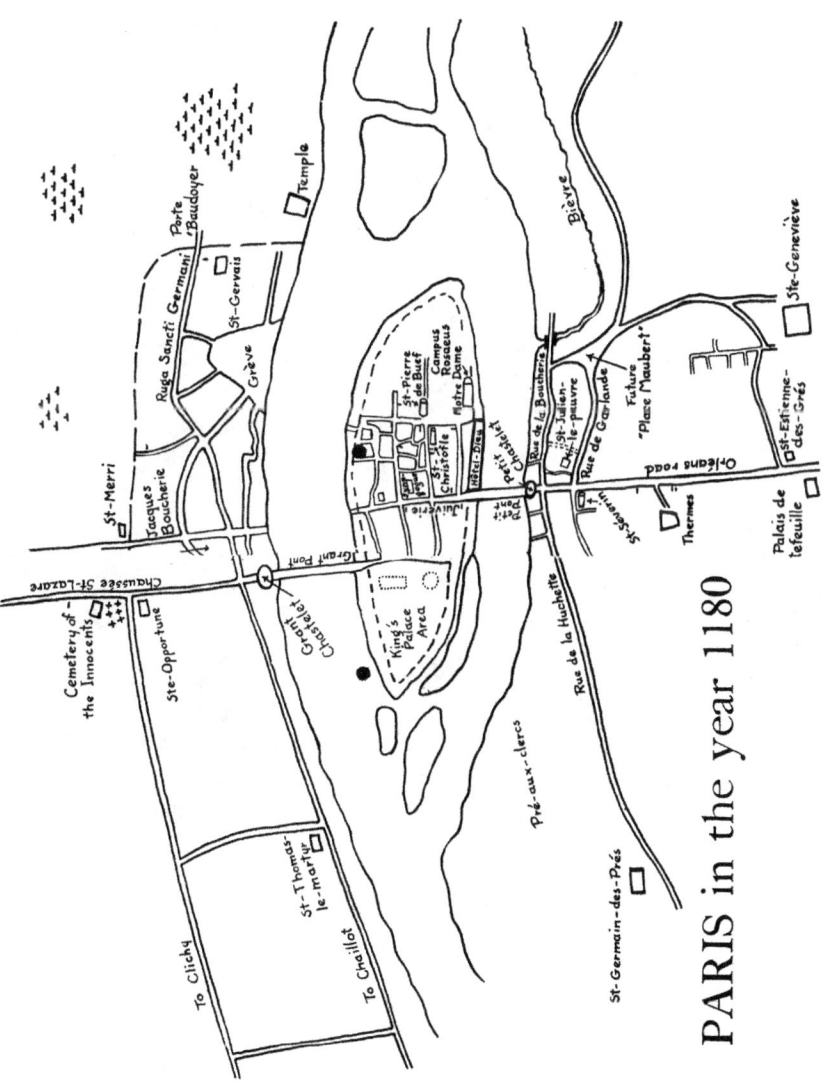

B: Map of Rome in the Middle Ages

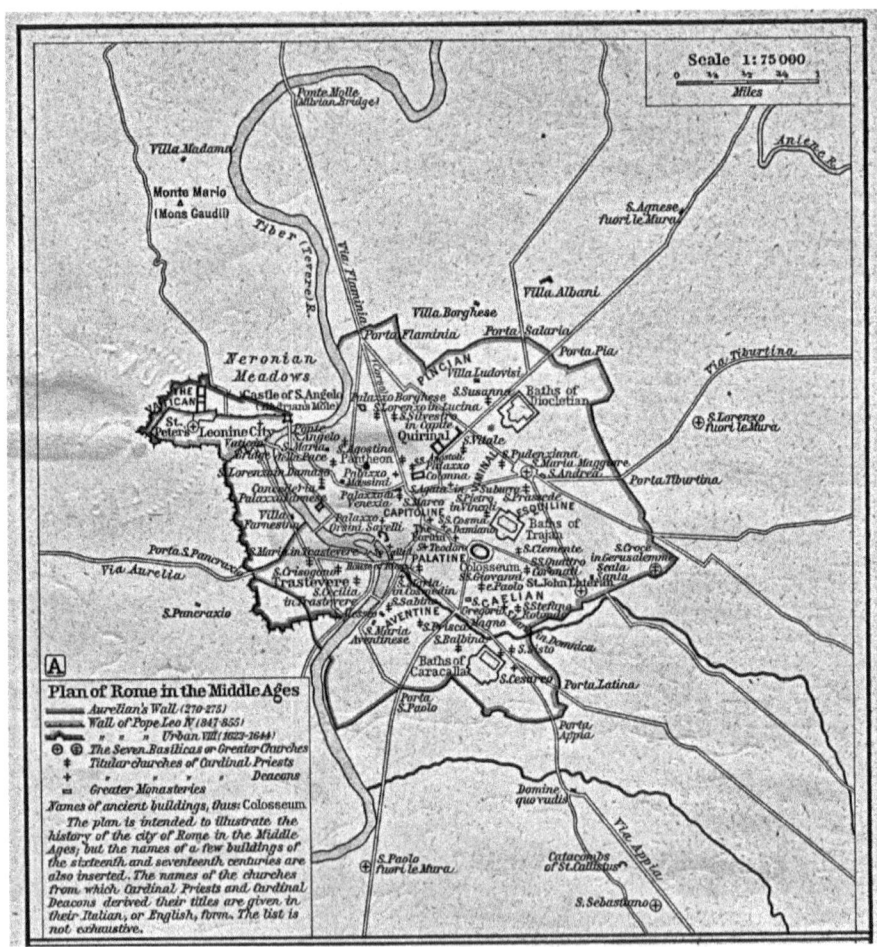

Historical Atlas by William Shepherd (1923-26). University of Texas at Austin
http://www.emersonkent.com/map_archive/rome_270.htm

Piazzalle Arnaldo, Brescia, Italy

Photo by Scatti & Bagagli

Monument to Arnold of Brescia by Odoardo Tabacchi (1831–1905), inaugurated 1882. The marble base was sculpted by Antonio Tagliaferri (1835–1909).

The inscription reads:
AD ARNALDO AL PRECURSORE AL MARTIRE DEL LIBERO ITALICO PENSIERO
BRESCIA SUA DECRETAVA TOSTO RIVENDICATA IN LIBERTA' MDCCCLX

IN HONOR OF ARNALDO, PRECURSOR AND MARTYR TO FREEDOM OF THOUGHT IN ITALY:
BRESCIA, BY DECREE, IS BOLDLY RECLAIMED IN LIBERTY. 1860
—TRANSLATED BY MARY PATTOCK.

Bust of Arnold in Gianicola, Rome

Photo by Jessica Spengler
SCULPTURE BY ODOARDO TABACCHI

Bibliography

Abaelardus, Petrus. *Dialectica.* Edited by L.M. DeRijk, PhD. Assen, Netherlands: Koninklijke Van Gorcum Comp. N.V., 1956.
Abailard, Peter. *Sic et Non.* Edited by Blanche B. Boyer and Richard McKeon. London: The University Press, 1967.
Abelard, Peter. *A Dialogue of a Philosopher with a Jew, and a Christian.* Translated by Pierre J. Payer. Toronto Ontario, Canada: Pontifical Institute of Mediaeval Studies, 1979.
———. *Opera omni.* Edited by J.P. Migne. *Patrologiae Latinae.* Turnholti: Typographi Brepols Editores Pontificii, 1967.
———. *The Letters of Peter Abelard Beyond the Personal.* Translated by Jan M. Ziolkowski. Washington, DC: The Catholic University of America Press, 2008.
———. *The Story of My Misfortunes. (Historia Calamitas).* Translated by Henry Adams Bellows. London: Collier Macmillan Publishers, Second Printing, 1976.
Abelard, Peter and Heloise d' Argenteuil. *The Letters of Abelard and Heloise.* Translated by Betty Radice. New York: Penguin, 1974.
Alfieri, Giovanni Teccani Degli. *Storia Di Brescia.* Brescia: Per Intreressamento Della Banca S. Paolo Di Brescia Morcelliana Editrice, 1961.
Almedingen, Edith M. *The English Pope (Adrian IV).* London: Heath Cranton, 1925.
Baker, Derek and Rosalind M.T. Hill, eds. *Medieval Women.* Oxford: Blackwell for the Ecclesiastical History Society, 1978.
Balzani, Ugo. *The Popes and the Hohenstaufen.* London: Longmans, Green, and Co., 1909.
Benson, Robert L. and Giles Constable, eds. *Renaissance and Renewal in the Twelfth Century.* Cambridge, MA: Harvard University Press, 1982.
Berman, Harold J. "Religious Foundations of Law in the West: An Historical Perspective." In *Journal of Law and Religion.* 1 1 (1983), 3–43.
Bernard of Clairvaux. *Five Books on Consideration: Advice to a Pope.* Translated by John D. Anderson & Elizabeth T. Kennan. Original title: *De consideratione ad Eugenium papam tertiam libri quinque, In The Works of Bernard of Clairvaux,* Volume Thirteen. Kalamazoo, Michigan: Cistercian Publications, 1976.
———. *The Letters of St. Bernard of Clairvaux.* Translated by Bruno Scott James. Chicago: Henry Regnery Company, 1953.
———. *Saint Bernard on the Love of God.* Translated by Terence L. Connolly. Westminster, MD: The Newman Press, 1951.

BIBLIOGRAPHY

———. *Sermons for the Summer Season.* Translated by Beverly Mayne Kienzie. Kalamazoo, MI: Cistercian Publications, 1991.

———. *Sermons of Conversion.* Translated with an introduction by Marie-Bernard Said. Kalamazoo, MI: Cistercian Publications, 1981.

Bettenson, Henry, ed. *Documents of the Christian Church.* London: Oxford University, 1943. Ninth printing, 1961.

Bloch, Herbert. "The Schism of Anacletus II and the Glanfeuil Forgeries of Peter the Deacon of Monte Cassino." *Traditto.* 8 (1952), 159ff.

Breasted, Huth, and Harding. *European History Atlas.* Chicago: Denoyer-Geppert, 1961.

Brooke, Chistopher. *The Twelfth Century Renaissance.* New York: Harcourt, Brace, and World, 1969.

———. *Europe in the Central Middle Ages 962–1154.* New York: Holt, Rinehart and Winston, 1963.

Burge, James. *Heloise & Abelard: A New Biography.* New York: Harper Collins, 2003.

Cantor, Norman F. "The Crisis of Western Monasticism 1050–1130." In *American Historical Revue.* 66, 47–67, October, 1960.

Carlyle, Alexander J. *A History of Medieval Political Theory in the West.* Vol. IV. London, 1903.

———. "The Sources of Medieval Political Theory and Its Connection with Medieval Politics." In *American Historical Revue.* 19 (1913), 1–12.

Casartelli, L. C. "The English Pope." In *Dublin Revue.* 130 (1902), 77–110.

Cave, Roy C. and Herbert H. Coulson. *A Source Book for Medieval Economic History.* Milwaukee: Bruce Publishing, 1936.

Collingwood, R. G. *The Idea of History.* New York: A Galaxy Book. First English edition, 1946. First published by Galaxy Book, 1956.

Compayre, Gabriel. *Abelard and the Origins and Early History of Universities.* Edited by Nicholas Murray Butler. New York: Charles Scribner's Sons, 1907.

Conant, Kenneth John. *Carolingian and Romanesque Architecture 800 to 1200 (The Yale University Pelican History of Art).* Edited by Nicolaus Pevsner. Great Britain: Pelican, 1959.

Coulton, George Gordon. *Five Centuries of Religion.* Cambridge: The University Press, 1927.

———. *Medieval Panorama.* Cleveland: Meridian Books, World Publishing, 1955.

———. *Studies in Medieval Thought.* New York: Russell & Russell, 1965.

Cowie, L. W. and John Selwyn Gummer. *The Christian Calendar.* London: Weidenfeld and Nicolson, 1974.

Daniel-Rops, Henri. *Bernard of Clairvaux: The Story of the Last of the Great Church Fathers.* Introduction by Thomas Merton. New York: Hawthorn Book, 1964.

Davenport, Basil, ed. *The Portable Roman Reader: The Culture of the Roman State.* New York: Penguin, 1951.

Davison, Ellen Scott. *Forerunners of Saint Francis and Other Studies.* Edited by Gertrude R. B. Richards. Boston: Houghton Mifflin, the Riverside Press Cambridge, 1927.

Dickinson, J. C. *The Origins of the Austin Canons and Their Introduction into England.* London: S.P.C.K., 1950.

Downs, Norton, ed. *Basic Documents of Medieval History.* Princeton, NJ: D. Van Nostrand Company, 1959.

Foran, E. A. *The Augustinians from St. Augustine to the Union, 1256.* London: Burns Oates, 1938.

BIBLIOGRAPHY

Franke, Heinrich. *Arnold von Brescia und Zeit.* Zurich, 1825.
Frazee, Charles A. "The Origins of Clerical Celibacy in the Western Church." In *Church History.* 57 (1988), Supplement, 108-126.
Frugoni, Arsenio. *Arnold da Brescia, Nelle Fonti Del Secolo XII.* Rome: Nella Sede Dell' Instituto Palazzo Forromini, 1954.
Gibbons, Edward. *The History of the Decline and Fall of the Roman Empire.* Vol. 6. New York: Harper & Brothers, 1879.
Gies, Joseph and Frances. *Life in a Medieval City.* New York: Harper Colophon, 1969.
Giesebrecht, W. von. *Arnold von Brescia.* (n. p. Munich, 1873).
Gilson, Etienne. *The Spirit of Mediaeval Philosophy.* Translated by A. H. C. Downes. New York: Charles Scribner's Sons, 1936.
Goodrich, Norma Lorre. *Medieval Myths.* New York: A Mentor Book, Published by the New American Library, 1961.
Greenaway, George William. *Arnold of Brescia.* Cambridge: Cambridge University Press, 1931.
Greenaway Reviews: Brown, Sidney M. *American Historical Review* 37:790. *English Historical Review* 48:152. Schaff, David. *Church History* 1 2:167-168.
Gregorovius, Ferdinand. *History of the City of Rome in the Middle Ages.* Vol. IV. — Part II. Translated from the fourth German edition by Annie Hamilton. London: George Bell & Sons, 1896.
Grosvenor, Melville Bell, ed. *The Alps.* Washington DC: Published by the National Geographic Society, 1973.
Grundmann, Herbert. *Religious Movements in the Middle Ages.* Notre Dame, IN: University of Notre Dame Press, 1995.
Gunther. Ligurius. *De Rebus gestis Frederici Imp.* Edited by J. P. Migne, *Migne Patralogiae Latinae*, Vol. CCXII, 1855.
Hare, Augustus John Cuthbert. *The Cities of Northern Italy.* Volumes I and II. New York: Routledge, 1883.
Haskins, Charles Homer. *The Renaissance of the 12th Century.* Cleveland: Meridian Books, the World Publishing Company, 1927. First Meridian printing, 1957.
Hausrath, A. *Arnold von Brescia.* (n. p. Liepsig, 1891).
Hibbert, A. B. "The Origins of the Medieval Town Patricate." *Past and Present.* 3, Feb., (1963), 15-27.
Highet, Gilbert. *Poets in a Landscape.* New York: Alfred A. Knoph, 1957.
Hoffman, J. Wesley. "The Commerce of the German Alpine Passes During the Early Middle Ages." *Journal of Political Economy* 31:826-839, Dec., 1923.
Holmes, George Andrew. *Later Middle Ages 1272-1485.* Edinburgh: T. Nelson, 1962.
Holmes, Urban Tigner Jr. *Daily Living in the Twelfth Century: Based on the Observations of Alexander Neckham in London and Paris.* Madison, WI: The University of Wisconsin Press, 1952.
Huizinga, J. *The Waning of the Middle Ages.* New York: Doubleday Anchor Books, Doubleday & Company, first published 1924, Anchor edition, 1954.
Hyman, Arthur & James J. Walsh, eds. *Philosophy in the Middle Ages.* Indianapolis: Hackett Publishing Company, 1973.
Jaffe, Philipp, ed. *Bibliotheca Rerum Germanicarum, Vol. I, Monumenta Corbeiensia,* 404:539-543. Berlin: Scientia Verlag Aalen, 1964.
James, Bruno Scott. *Saint Bernard of Clairvaux.* London: Hodder & Stoughton, 1957.

BIBLIOGRAPHY

Jenkyns, Richard. *Classical Literature, An Epic Journey from Homer to Virgil and Beyond.* New York: Basic Books, 2016.

John of Salisbury. *Historiae Pontificalis Quae Supersunt, (Memoirs of the Papal Court).* Edited with introduction by Reginald L. Poole. Oxford: At the Clarendon Press, MCMXXVII.

———. *The Historia Pontificalis of John of Salisbury.* Edited and translated with an introduction by Marjorie Chibnall. New York: Thomas Nelson and Sons, 1956.

———. *Frivolities of Courtiers and Footprints of Philosophers.* Being a translation of the 1st, 2nd and Selections from the 7th and 8th books of the *Policratus.* Translated by Joseph B. Pike. Minneapolis: U. of M., 1938.

———. *Opera Omnia. Patralogiae Latinae* 199. Edited by J. P. Migne. Petit-Montroughe, 1855.

Jusserand, J. J. *English Wayfaring Life in the Middle Ages.* Translated from French by Lucy Toulmin Smith. New York: Barnes and Noble, 1st pub. 1889, 4th Edition, 1950.

Kantorowicz, Ernst H. "Pro Patria Mori in Medieval Political Thought." In *American Historical Revue.* 56:472–492, Apr., 1951.

Knowles, David. *Christian Monasticism.* World University Library, New York: McGraw-Hill, 1969.

———. *The Evolution of Medieval Thought.* Baltimore: Helicon, 1962.

Kruger, Hilmar C. "The Wares of Exchange in the Genoese-African Traffic of the Twelfth Century." *Speculum* 12:57–71, Jan., 1937.

Kuttner, Stephan, "The Revival of Jurisprudence." In Benson, Robert L. and Giles Constable, eds. *Renaissance and Renewal in the Twelfth Century,* 299–223. Cambridge, MA: Harvard, 1982.

Langdon, Helen, ed. *The Knopf Traveler's Guide to Art—Italy.* New York: Alfred A. Knopf, 1984.

Leff, Gordon. *Medieval Thought: St Augustine to Ockham.* Baltimore, MD: Penguin, 1958.

Livingstone, Elizabeth, ed. *The Concise Oxford Dictionary of the Christian Church.* Oxford: Oxford University Press, 1977.

Lucas, Angela M. *Women in the Middle Ages.* New York: St. Martin's, 1983.

Luscombe, D. E. *The School of Peter Abelard.* Cambridge: At the University Press, 1969.

Mabillon, Jean. *Life and Works of Saint Bernard: Abbot of Clairvaux.* Volumes 1 and 2. Translated and edited with additional notes by Samuel J. Eales. London: Hodges, 1889.

Madden, Thomas F. *Empires of Trust,* New York: Dutton, 2008.

Mann, Horace K. *Lives of the Popes in the Middle Ages.* London: Kegan Paul, Trench, Trubner & Co., 1929.

———. *Nicholas Breadspear (Hadrian IV).* St. Louis, MO: B. Herder, 1914.

Map, Walter. *De Nugis Curialium, (Courtiers' Trifles).* [Translated] by Frederick Tupper and Marbury Bladen Oghle. London: Chatto & Windus, 1924.

McCallum, J. Ramsay. *Abelard's Christian Theology.* Oxford: Basil and Blackwell, 1948.

———. *Abelard's Ethics.* Oxford: Basil and Blackwell, 1935.

Mews, Constants J. *Abelard and Heloise.* New York: Oxford University Press, 2005.

———. "The Council of Sens (1141): Abelard, Bernard, and the Fear of Social Upheaval," *Speculum* 77 (2002): 342–82.

———. *The Lost Love Letters of Heloise and Abelard.* New York: St. Martin's Press 1999.

Michelin, *Italy.* 7th Edition, London: The Dicken's Press, 1969.

Milman, H. H. *History of Latin Christianity IV.* 3rd Edition. London, 1883.

Bibliography

Murray, A. Victor. *Abelard and St Bernard: A study in twelfth century 'modernism'.* New York: Manchester University Press, Barnes & Noble, 1967.

Nietzche, Friedrich. *The Use and Abuse of History.* New York: The Liberal Arts Press, 1957.

Otto of Freising. *The Two Cities, A Chronicle of Universal History to the Year 1146 A. D.* (*Chronicon seu historia de duabus civitatibus*). Translated in full with Introduction and Notes by Charles Christopher Mierow. Edited by Austin P. Evans and Charles Knapp. New York: Octagon Books, 1966.

_____. *The Deeds of Frederick Barbarossa* (*Gesta Friderici I Imperatoris*). Translated and annotated with an introduction by Charles Christopher Mierow. New York; Columbia University Press, 1953.

Pirenne, Henri. *Economic and Social History of Medieval Europe.* Translated from the French by I. E. Clegg. New York: A Harvest Book, Harcourt, Brace and Company, 1st published 1933, 1st U. S. edition, 1937.

_____. *Medieval Cities: Their Origins and the Revival of Trade.* Translated by Frank D. Halsey. Garden City, NY: Doubleday Anchor Books, Doubleday, 1956.

Poole, Reginald Lane. *Illustrations of the History of Medieval Thought.* London and Edinburgh: Williams and Norgate, MDCCCLXXXIV and 2nd edition, revised, 1920, New York: Dover.

_____. *Studies in Chronology and History.* Oxford: At the Clarendon Press, 1934.

Postan, M. M. and H. J. Habakkuk, eds. *The Cambridge Economic History of Europe.* Vol. II, *Trade and Industry in the Middle Ages.* Cambridge: At the University Press, 1952.

Postan, M. M., E.E. Rich, and Edward Miller, Editors. *The Cambridge Economic History of Europe.* Vol. 3, *Economic Organization and Policies in the Middle Ages.* Cambridge: At the University Press, 1963.

Power, Eileen. *Medieval People.* Garden City, NY: Doubleday Anchor Books, Doubleday, 1956.

_____. *Medieval Women.* Edited by M. M. Postan. Cambridge: Cambridge University Press, 1975.

Rashdall, Hastings. *The Universities of Europe in the Middle Ages.* Edited by F. M. Powicke and A. B. Eindon, Vol. I. Oxford: Oxford University Press, 1st edition, 1895. new edition, 1936.

Reinke, Darrel R. "'Austin's Labour': Patterns of Governance in Medieval Augustinian Monasticism." *Church History* 56, 157–171, June, 1987.

Rowe, John Gordon. "Papacy and the Greeks." *Church History* 28:115–130, Sept., 1959.

Roth, Cecil. "The Popes and the Jews." In *Church Quarterly Review* 123:75–92, Oct., 1936.

Runciman, Stephen. *Byzantine Civilization.* Cleveland and New York: Meridian Books, The World Publishing Company, 1933, 8th printing, 1964.

St. Possidius, Bishop of Calama. "The Life of Saint Aurelius Augustine, the Bishop of Hippo." In Foran, E. A. *The Augustinians* 1–36. London: Burns Oates & Washbourne Ltd., 1938.

Sanford, Eva Matthews. "The Lombard Cities, Empire, and Papacy in a Cleveland Manuscript." In *Speculum* 12:203–208, Apr., 1937.

Sikes, J. G. *Peter Abailard.* New York: Russell & Russell, 1965.

Southern, R. W. *The Making of the Middle Ages.* New Haven, CT: Yale University Press, 1953.

_____. *Western Society and the Church in the Middle Ages.* New York: Penguin Books, 1970.

Stevenson, J., ed. *A New Eusebius.* London: S P C K, 1957.

Bibliography

Sturzo, Luigi. "Papacy and Empire from St. Bernard to Dante." In *Dublin Review* 195:25–45, July, 1934.

Tanner, J. R., Previte-Orton, C. W., and Brooke, Z. N. eds. *The Cambridge Medieval History. Volume V., Contest of Empire and Papacy.* Planned by J. B. Bury. New York: The Macmillan Company, 1926.

Tierney, Brian. *The Crisis of Church and State 1050–1300.* Englewood Cliffs, N. J.: Prentice-Hall, 1964.

The Bergamese Poet. "*Gesta di federico primi in Italia.*" Translated by Mary Martin McLaughin. In Ross, James Bruce and Mary Martin McLaughlin, Editors. *The Portable Medieval Reader*, 341–344. New York: Viking, 1960.

Thompson, James Westfall and Johnson, Edgar Nathaniel. *An Introduction to Medieval Europe 300–1500.* New York: W. W. Norton, 1937.

Thompson, James Westfall. *Economic and Social History of the Middle Ages.* Volumes I and II. New York: Frederick Ungar Publishing, 1928 (republished 1959).

Treece, Henry. *The Crusades.* New York: Random House, 1962.

Ullman, Walter. "A Medieval Document on Papal Theories of Government." *English Historical Review.* 61:180–201, May, 1946.

_____. *Principles of Government and Politics in the Middle Ages.* New York: Barnes and Noble, 1966.

Van Bavel, Tarsicius J., ed. *The Rule of Saint Augustine.* Translated by Raymond Canning. Garden City, NY: Image Books, A Division of Doubleday, 1986.

Volz, Carl A. *The Church of the Middle Ages: Growth and Change from 600 to 1400.* Saint Louis: Concordia Publishing House, 1970.

Von Hagen, Victor W. *The Roads that Led to Rome.* Cleveland, OH: The World Publishing Company, 1967.

Waddell, Helen. *Peter Abelard*, A Novel. New York: The Literary Guild, 1933.

_____. *The Wandering Scholars.* Garden City, NY: Doubleday, 1961. First published in 1927.

Webb, Clement C. J. *John of Salisbury.* Methuen and Co. Ltd., 1932. Reissued, New York: Russell and Russell, 1971.

Weiser, Francis X. *Handbook of Christian Feasts and Customs.* New York: Harcourt Brace, 1952. Imprimatur Feb. 5, 1958.

White, Hayden V. "The Gregorian Ideal and St. Bernard of Clairvaux." In *Journal of the History of Ideas.* 21:321–346, July, 1960.

Whitney, James Ponder. "The Reform of the Church", Chapter I in *The Cambridge Medieval History. Volume V., Contest of Empire and Papacy.* Edited by Tanner, J. R., C.W. Previte-Orton, and Z. N. Brooke. Planned by J. B. Bury. New York: Macmillan, 1926.

Williams, Watkin. *The Mysticism of S. Bernard of Clairvaux.* London: Burns Oates & Washbourne Ltd., Publishers to the Holy See, 1931.

Zeller, Jules. *Les Tribuns et Les Revolutions en Italie.* "Arnaud de Brescia." 81–145. Paris: Librairie Academique Didier et Cie, Libraires-Editeurs, 1874.

Zema, Demetrius B. "The Houses of Tuscany and Pierleone in the Crisis of Rome in the Eleventh Century." In *Traditto* 2:155–175.

Index

Abelard, Peter, ix, xii, xv, 17, 20, 24, teaching in Paris, 25–42; his passion for the life of learning and the art of dialectic, 32; his love of the philosophers, 33; the great divide with Augustine, 34; *Sic et Non*, 35; the Realist/Nominalist debate, 38; Conceptualism, 39; the function of logic, 40; impact on Arnold, 56; joined at Mont Sainte Geneviève by Arnold, 61–63; Council of Sens, 64–77; last days with Peter the Venerable, 78; 80, 82, 83, 107, 112, 120, 122, 125, John of Salisbury's reference to Peter's friendship with Arnold, 128; Otto of Freising's reference to Peter being Arnold's teacher, 130; attacked by Bernard in his letters, 132–133; discussion of Arnold's studies with him, 147–149; relationship with Heloise, 150–156

Adrian (Hadrian) IV, xvi, 6; puts Rome under interdict and exiles Arnold, 109–114; the crowning of Frederick Barbarossa, 115–118; 122, 123, 126, 129, 130

Anacletas (Anti-Pope), 48, 50, 93, 95

Anastasius IV, 109

Anselm of Canterbury, 27

Anselm of Laon, 26

Arnold of Brescia, vi, ix, xi, xv, 2, 5, studies in Paris, 25–42; at San Pietro and in Brescia, 43–60; his convictions: the rule regarding community goods, 51; relinquishing temporal power by the church, 53; elevating the laity, 54; teaching on the sacraments of baptism and communion, 56; on the move, 61–83: Milan, 62; Paris, 63; Council of Sens, 64; teaching on Mont Sainte Geneviève, 77; teaching in Zurich, 79; in Passau, 82; Pastor of Rome, 84–113: reconciliation with Eugenius III, 87; break with Eugenius, 89; alignment with the commune and pastor of Rome, 95; pastor of the Republic, Phase II, 99–113: pact with the Senate, 99; Arnold's position, 107; exile, 109; martyr, 114–127: final witness, 118; the poet's questions for Arnold, 120; questions and considerations, 122; Primary sources regarding Arnold, 127–139: John of Salisbury, 127; Otto of Freising, 129; Bernard of Clairvaux, 132; The Bergamese Poet, 137; Walter Map, 139; Letter to Fredrick, 140; Student days with Peter Abelard examined, 147–149; statues by Odoardo Tabacci: Piazzalle Arnaldo, 159; Gianacola, Rome, 160

Augustine, 6, 15, 32, 33, on original sin, 34–35; 37, promotes common life, 44–53; 54, view of baptism compared to Abelard, 56–58; 63, 73

Index

Augustinian (Austin) canons regular, x, 3, purpose, 15–17; 27, 29, origins, 43–52; 63, 79, 80, 82, 96, 111, 124, 148

Benson, Robert, 18, 93, 102, 103, 108

Berengar of Poitiers, 68, "Apologeticus," 69, 72

Bergamese Poet (The), vi, 55, 62, 119, 121, account of Arnold's martyrdom, 137–139

Bernard of Clairvaux, xii, xv, 14, 17, 34, 36, 50, 54, 55, 57, 62, activities regarding the Council of Sens, 64–77; 78, 79, 80–81, attempt to influence Cardinal Guido, 82–83; concerns about making Bernard of Pisa (Eugenius III) pope 84–91; supports Innocent III, promotes Second Crusade, opposes commune of Rome, 95–100; apologia on the plight of Jerusalem and failure of the Crusade, 98; 105, 119, 120, 125, 126, 128, letters regarding Arnold of Brescia, 132–137; 139, 147–149, visits Heloise, 156

Catullus, 2

Canossa—Countess Matilda, 11

Concordat of Worms, 13

Cistercians, 3, 16, 17, 47, 80, 90, 139

Conrad III, xvi, 49, 50, 80, 81, 85, 93, 95, 97, 98, letters of 1149 from the Roman Senate, 101–104; 129, 140

Council of Clermont—First Crusade, 1

Damian, Peter, 16, 45, 53, 63,

Donation of Constantine, 92, 106, 115

Eberhard of Bodman, xvi, 80, 107, 144

Eugenius III, Pope, xv, 79, reconciliation with Arnold, 83; 84, 85, Eugenius and Arnold, 86–91; activities as pope, 93–96; 98, excommunicates Arnold, 99; attacks the commune of Rome, 100–101; 103, 105, 108, 109, 125, 126, 127, 128, 131, 139, 149

Frederick Barbarossa (Frederick II, Holy Roman Emperor), xvi, 6, 20, 55, 62, 79, 80, Wezel's pastoral letter to Frederick, 104–107; 108, 109, 110, negotiations with Pope Adrian, crowned emperor, 114–118; 119, 121, 122, 123, 125, deeds of by Otto of Freising, 129–131, 137, 138, text of Wezel's letter to Frederick, 140–144; speech of Roman delegates and Frederick's response, 145–146

Geoffrey of Auxerre, 34, 67, 74

Geoffrey of Chartes, 65

Gerhoh of Reichersberg, 100, 120

Gilbert de la Porrée, 17, 68, 69, 73

Golias/Goliards, 18, 21, 22, 23, 76

Great St. Bernard Pass, 4, 16, 27, 63

Greenaway, William, 26, 42, 43, 62, 65, 75, 76, 77, 78, 79, 80, 81, 87, 99, 100, 102, 103, 104, 108, 109, 111, 114, 116, 149

Gregorovius, Ferdinand, 85, 87, 88, 91, 92, 93, 94, 100, 102, 103, 104, 108, 110, 111, 114, 116, 118, assessment of Arnold, 121–122; 149

Gregory I, Pope, 102

Gregory VI, Pope, 10

Gregory VII (Hildebrand), Pope, 11, 12, 16, 19, 26, 45, 53, 71

Guido, (Guy) Cardinal, papal legate to Passau, xv, 82, 83, 86, 88, 89, 125, 135

Guido of Puella, 100

Guido of St. Pudentiana, 110, 114

Index

Guy of Costello, Pope Celestine II, 68, 69, 83, 86

Haskins, Charles Homer, 18–21, 23, 31, 41, 91

Heloise d' Argenteuil, xii, 27, 42, 69, 71, 78, 125, Heloise and Peter, 150–156

Henry III, 9, 10

Henry IV, 2, 10, 11, 12

Henry Sanglier, Archbishop of Sens, 67–71

Herman, Bishop of Constance, 80, 81

Hyacinth Boboni, Pope Celestine III, 64, 68, 69, 75, 78, 79, 82, 128

Innocent II, xv, the Brescian uprising, 48–51; exiles Arnold, 60–62; 69, regarding the Council of Sens, 71–77; 82, 83, 86, 87, 88, 95, 125, 126, 128, 130, 131, 132, 135, 139

John of Salisbury, xii, 16, 34, 44, 51, 53, 54, 61, 62, 64, 68, 69, 73, 76, 77, 78, 79, 83, 86–89, 96, 98, 99, 103, 104, 106, 112, 125, entry about Arnold in *Historia Pontificalis*, 127–129; 130, 147, 148, 149

Leo IX, Pope, 10, 11, 12, 15

Louis VII, king, 68, 74, 78

Manfred, bishop of Brescia, versus the *patarin*, 48–50; obtains papal exile of Arnold 59– 62; 125

Map, Walter, 8, 17, 27, 44, 56, dinner hosted by Thomas Moore, 90–91; 95, text of Map's account, 139–140

Nominalism, 39, 40

Otto of Freising, xii, 6, 7, 14, 25, 41, 53, 54, 55, 56, 59, 69, 75, 79, 87, 107, 114, 117, 119, 125, on Arnold, 129, 130; account of exchanges between the Romans and Frederick II, 144–146; 147, 148, 149

patarin, 43, 44, 48, 49, 60, 63

Peter the Venerable, 14, 24, 53, 77, 78, 125, 156

Pierleone, Jordan, 93, 94, 101

Pirenne, Henri, 7, 8

Possidius, 52, 53

Realism, 38–40, 122

Roger of Sicily, 90, 100, 102, 110

Roscelin, 26, 39, 41

Rudolf of Ravensburg, 80, 144

Sic et non, 20, 30, 32, 33, brief description, 35–37; 41, 56, 58, 59, 70

simony, described, 9–11; 14, 49, 63, 106, 143

Stephen, bishop of Paris, 66, 67, 78

Ulrich of Lenzburg, 80, 81, 107, 144

Wezel (Wetzel), 79, 80, discussion of his letter to Frederick, 104–107; 115, text of letter, 140–144

Wibald of Stablo and Corvey, 80, 102, 103, 104, letter from Pope Eugenius III, 107–109; 140

William I of Sicily, 110

William of Champeaux, 26, 39

William of St. Thierry, 34, letter to Bernard of Clairvaux alleging heresy in Abelard's *Theologia*, 65–66; 72

www.ingramcontent.com/pod-product-compliance
Lightning Source LLC
Chambersburg PA
CBHW071232170426
43191CB00032B/1350